Creativity, Education and the Arts

Series editor
Anne Harris
Royal Melbourne Institute of Technology
Melbourne, Australia

This series emerges out of recent rapid advances in creativity- and arts-informed research in education that seeks to reposition creativity studies within (and in conversation with) education as a multi- and interdisciplinary field.

This series takes as its starting point the interrelationship between arts-based research and a growing neuroscientific, cultural and economic discourse of creativity and creative industries, and the need for education to play a larger role in these expanding discourses. It also takes as a priori an invitation to creativity scholars to move more robustly into theorizing the work of arts- and creativity-based research work, bridging a historical gap between 'science' and 'art', between 'theoretical' and 'applied' approaches to research, and between qualitative and quantitative research paradigms.

The following are the primary aims of the series:

- To publish creativity research and theory in relation to education (including schools, curriculum, policy, higher education, pedagogy, learning and teaching, etc.).
- To put education at the heart of debates on creativity, re-establish the significance of creativity for learning and teaching and development analyses, and forge links between creativity and education.
- To publish research that draws on a range of disciplinary and theoretical lenses, strengthening the links between creative and arts education and geographies, anthropology, creative industries, aesthetics and philosophy, history, and cultural studies.
- To publish creativity research and theory with an international scope that explores and reflects the current expansion of thought and practice about global flows, cultural heritage, and creativity and the arts in education.

More information about this series at
http://www.springer.com/series/14926

Chris McRae · Aubrey Huber

Creating Performances for Teaching and Learning

A Practice Session for Pedagogy

Chris McRae
Department of Communication
University of South Florida
Tampa, FL, USA

Aubrey Huber
Department of Communication
University of South Florida
Tampa, FL, USA

Creativity, Education and the Arts
ISBN 978-3-319-54560-8   ISBN 978-3-319-54561-5   (eBook)
DOI 10.1007/978-3-319-54561-5

Library of Congress Control Number: 2017939107

Cover image: © Halfpoint/iStock/Getty Images

Printed on acid-free paper

This Palgrave Macmillan imprint is published by Springer Nature
The registered company is Springer International Publishing AG
The registered company address is: Gewerbestrasse 11, 6330 Cham, Switzerland

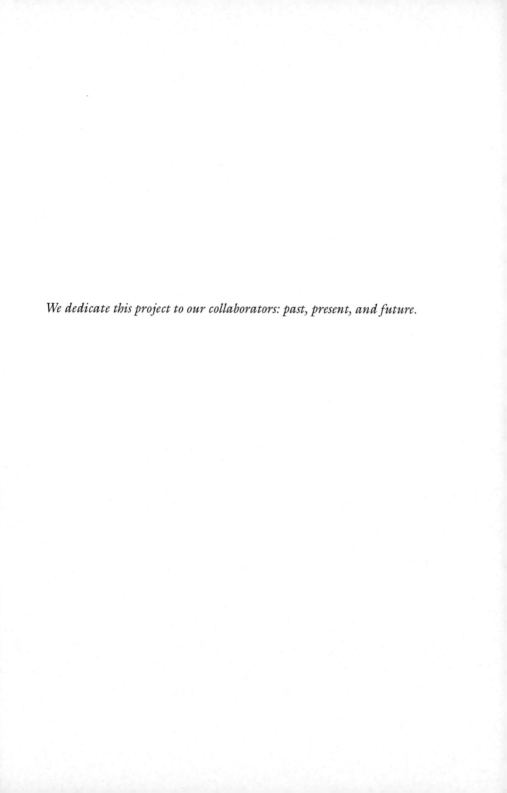

We dedicate this project to our collaborators: past, present, and future.

ACKNOWLEDGEMENTS

After a collaborative performance presentation at a national conference our friend, mentor, and colleague, Amy Kilgard, met us in the back of the room and kindly complimented our performance. She told us that she especially appreciated the way we often worked and presented together. She went on to explain that what she appreciated most about this kind of collaborative presentation (in addition to the content of our work) was the way we put on display the fact that all of our work (as scholars) is always already some kind of collaboration. This comment reflects an important ethic that informs this project: First, our work as researchers, teachers, and artists is only ever possible because of others. And second, our work here is a collaboration in the broadest possible sense. Acknowledging, even if only partially, the others who make this book possible is an opportunity both to express our gratitude for these people, and to articulate and name some of the people and relationships who we are lucky to count as collaborators.

We would therefore like to acknowledge and thank our teachers who exemplify for us what it means to commit to, theorize, and practice liberatory pedagogy. First, we both thank our teacher, friend, and mentor, Stacy Holman Jones. We are grateful to Stacy for her continued enthusiasm for and dedication to performance scholarship, and her everlasting encouragement of our work. Stacy is not only our teacher and mentor, she demonstrates for us what it means to be a scholar-practitioner who is not only committed to her work, but to others. We thank Stacy for introducing us to the thoughtful reader, and generous scholar, Anne Harris. We appreciate Anne's support of this project, and we are grateful to her for opening up space for us in the Creativity, Education, and the Arts series.

We thank Karen Mitchell who introduced Aubrey to Performance Studies through her activist forum theater troupe, SAVE (Students Against a Violent Environment), and Elizabeth Bell, Marcyrose Chvasta, and Michael LeVan who enacted teacher–performer–activists for Chris during his time as a student at the University of South Florida. Similarly, we are grateful for the faculty at Southern Illinois University (SIU), who introduced us to critical performance pedagogy and helped us develop our identities as teacher-scholars. Specifically, we thank our dissertation advisors, Nathan Stucky and Ron Pelias, for offering us thoughtful, gracious examples of scholarly collaboration and mentorship throughout our degree programs and beyond. We are thankful for the careful interpretative, critical, and performance pedagogies modeled for us by Nilanjana Bardhan, Ross Singer, Suzanne Daughton, Lenore Langsdorf, Satoshi Toyosaki, Craig Gingrinch-Philbrook, Jonny Gray, and Sandy Pensoneau-Conway. We are also grateful to our friend and mentor Kathy Hytten, whose commitment to critical and social justice pedagogies are invaluable to us in our writing, teaching, and scholarly collaboration.

Our understanding and application of critical performance pedagogy would not be possible without Elyse Pineau. We were lucky to find her scholarship, and even more fortunate to experience her direction on stage and in the classroom. We also greatly appreciate the impact of our late teacher, mentor, and friend, John T. Warren, for cultivating our interest in critical and performance pedagogies, for the various introductions to scholars and practitioners that continue to influence our work, and most of all, for teaching us how to take seriously our classrooms as essential sites of research. His pedagogy and scholarship continues to serve as a springboard for our individual and collaborative work.

By extension of what we learn from our teachers, we want to acknowledge the scholars and friends who continue to shape our teaching and scholarship. Thank you Amy Kilgard, Keith Nainby, Deanna Fassett, Deanna Shoemaker, Abe Kahn, Jeanine Minge, Tony Adams, Jillian Tullis, Heather Hull, Mike Garvin, and Danielle Dick McGeough.

In acknowledging those who have taught us, we would be remiss if we did not also take time to thank the students who not only teach us how to be teachers, but who also are our collaborators. Without the efforts of students, we would be unable to document and theorize peda-gogical settings or fully develop our ideas for the "practice session." We would like to acknowledge the students who have taken classes with us, specifically our undergraduate performance classes, and our gradu-ate classes. We would also like to thank the undergraduate and graduate students who engaged in our first collaborative performance workshop, "Speech Acts!" Particularly, we want to express our appreciation to Alyse Keller. We are grateful to Alyse for collaborating with us in performance workshops, working with us in classes, and for caring for our son so we could make time to work on this project together.

This book would not have been possible without the support and col-laboration of our families. It is likely our parents were the first people who taught us about the value and necessity of collaboration in giving us the most precious gifts we could have received as first-born children: siblings. We greatly appreciate what we learned about collaboration from growing up and engaging with our siblings and their partners, Danny, Michelle, Mandy, Zach, Katy, and Chris. As we are now parents our-selves, we so value the collaborations of our parents. We want to also acknowledge our parents' continued commitment to collaborating with us as they have spent countless hours charming and caring for our son during this project. Laurie and Randy, Bob and Lyn, this project is made possible by your love and support. Thank you.

Lastly, we want to acknowledge the impact and importance of the col-laborations that emerge from our interactions with our son Graham. He teaches us daily about the critical value of creativity, imagination, and play. We also look forward to the collaborations that are yet to come with the newest member of our family, Oliver.

CONTENTS

1   Introduction: Creating Performances
    for Teaching and Learning   1

2   Practice Space   15

3   Performance as Research   43

4   Music and Routine   71

5   Crafting Pictures and Reflexivity   97

6   Writing and Experimentation   127

7   Future Sessions   155

Index   183

Series Editor's Introduction

Teaching and Learning as Critical Performative Encounter

It is with great pleasure that I welcome Chris McRae and Aubrey Huber's beautiful new text into the Palgrave Macmillan series *Creativity, Education and the Arts*. My intention in establishing this series was to highlight the interdisciplinary nature of much creativity education work, which tends to often remain outside of the "creative conversation" of creative and cultural industries, performance studies, youth studies, art history and aesthetics, and even at times the Deleuzian turn in theorizing creativity and practice led research. I knew creativities research in education to be robust and long-standing (Craft 2004; Jeffrey and Craft 2004; Burnard 2007; Cremin et al. 2006; Thomson and Sefton-Green 2010; Sefton-Green et al. 2011; Harris 2014, 2016), if still somewhat of a loner. This series' express intention is not to suggest that work is not being done at this intersection, but to highlight it and bring it into conversation with other disciplines. This latest book by Chris McRae and Aubrey Huber represents another important expansion of scholarship on creativity and its educative power, this time into the fields of performance studies, critical pedagogy and communication theory. It represents new extensions by emerging scholars of well-established scholarship at their own intersections of these areas, and I congratulate them on this dynamic and innovative contribution. It goes without saying that I also once again extend my gratitude to Palgrave Macmillan and in particular to editor Eleanor Christie for her commitment and support to continuing to champion and expand this book series, as well as expertly shepherd new works like this current text from McRae and Huber.

These authors invite us into their world through the evocative opening describing their hot autumn graduate school days in southern Illinois, and their simultaneous awakening into both a love of critical performance pedagogies, and into a rich and sustained collaboration with one another. They extend Elyse Pineau's pivotal work on critical performative pedagogy (2002, 2005) and theorize a new application for that work which brings us into palpable touch with classrooms and performances spaces in this second decade of the twenty-first century. For them, as for Pineau, embodiment is central to the educative, the political and the creative cause.

The growing body of scholarly research into critical performance and pedagogy (in its many forms including work by Denzin 2009; Alexander et al. 2004; McLaren and Kincheloe 2007; Madison and Hamera 2006) is now well established and thoroughly interdisciplinary. McRae and Huber's text provides a welcome expansion of this body of work. In addition to its important focus on the critical (including gender, race, and socio-economic), this book documents the authors' commitment to process and embodiment, as well as the summative outputs which result. Such a rich text only eventuates from the kind of decade-long collaboration that these two co-authors use as the basis of their present enquiry.

While all texts included in this series fit the mandate of the creativity–education–arts intersection, this text's foregrounding of embodied performance as a kind of processual teaching and learning together is a masterful example of how education, at its best, is both a *doing* and an event, a *becoming* and a product, a mutual relationship always in the context of a critical social, political and historical moment, in which we are all simultaneously the performer/audience, teacher/student, and changer/changed.

One major innovation of this book concerns the authors' decision to structure it as a series of "practice sessions," a familiar notion to any musical or theatre performer, yet combined cleverly with the format of a lesson plan it is transformed into a user-friendly modeling of the kinds of critical creative approaches the authors are advocating here for bringing performance into any kinds of classroom situation. This combination offers a literal and metaphoric starting place for readers to develop our own sessions and extend the work provided—another reminder that this text is a tool that the co-authors wish us to use, not just read and put away. McRae and Huber offer practical and helpful examples, an offering as would happen in an improvisation or collaborative performance relationship. All of these unique features contribute to this book's strength and its authors' commitment and constant return to the methods and principles of performance as research, as readers become a part of this community and set of practices on every page.

I congratulate McRae and Huber for their beautiful work and important alignment with the mandate of this series, going far beyond the highlighting of intersections between education, creativity, and the arts, and making us think expansively about the varying ways that classrooms can become sites for creative innovation. McRae and Huber's book does this in both formal and informal ways, firstly through their chapter structure which targets explicit "pedagogical practices and creative acts." Yet beyond the explicit, there is an implicit modeling and enacting of the theory and practice (praxis) here that will show readers just how to pursue the goals these authors articulate. And now, more than ever, we need lived and usable examples of how to move forward creatively and critically, in formal and informal learning spaces, with relational and embodied attention to social change. That is what you will find in this book, and I'm so pleased to include it in this series.

Melbourne, Australia
January 2017

Anne Harris

REFERENCES

Alexander, B. K., Anderson, G. L., & Gallegos, B. (Eds.). (2004). *Performance theories in education: Power, pedagogy, and the politics of identity*. NY: Routledge.

Burnard, P. (2007). Reframing creativity and technology: Promoting pedagogic change in music education. *Journal of Music, Technology & Education, 1*(1), 37–55.

Craft, A. (2003). *Creativity across the primary curriculum: Framing and developing practice*. Routledge.

Cremin, T., Burnard, P., & Craft, A. (2006). Pedagogy and possibility thinking in the early years. *Thinking skills and creativity, 1*(2), 108–119.

Denzin, N. K. (2009). A critical performance pedagogy that matters. *Ethnography and Education*, *4*(3), 255–270.

Harris, Anne. 2016. *Creativity and Education*. London: Palgrave Macmillan.

Harris, Anne. 2014. *The Creative Turn*. Rotterdam: Sense.

Jeffrey, B., & Craft, A. (2004). Teaching creatively and teaching for creativity: distinctions and relationships. *Educational studies*, *30*(1), 77–87.

Madison, D. S., & Hamera, J. (Eds.) (2006). *The Sage handbook of performance studies*. Thousand Oaks, CA: Sage.

McLaren, P., & Kincheloe, J. L. (2007). *Critical pedagogy: Where are we now?* (Vol. 299). New York, NY: Peter Lang.

Pineau, E. L. (2002). Critical performative pedagogy: Fleshing out the politics of liberatory education. In N. Stucky & C. Wimmer (Eds.), *Teaching performance studies* (pp. 41–54). Carbondale, IL: Southern Illinois University Press.

Pineau, E. L. (2005). Teaching is performance: Reconceptualizing a problematic metaphor. In B. K. Alexander, G. L. Anderson, & B. P. Gallegos (Eds.), *Performance theories in education: Power, pedagogy, and the politics of identity* (pp. 15–39). Mahwah, NJ: Lawrence Erlbaum Associates.

Sefton-Green, J., Thomson, P., Jones, K., & Bresler, L. (Eds.). (2011). *The Routledge international handbook of creative learning*. Routledge.

Thomson, P., & Sefton-Green, J. (Eds.). (2010). *Researching creative learning: Methods and issues*. Routledge.

OTHER BOOKS IN THIS SERIES

Creativity and Education (2016)
Anne Harris
Creative Methods for Engaging and Encountering the Drama in Teacher Leadership (2016)
Jerome Cranston and Kristin Kusanovich
Knowledge, Creativity and Failure: A new pedagogical framework for creative arts education (2016)
Chris Hay
Critical Autoethnography, Performance and Pedagogy (2017)
Stacy Holman Jones & Marc Pruyn (Eds)

CHAPTER 1

Introduction: Creating Performances for Teaching and Learning

We first met in 2007. The summer had been a hot one and the fall semester promised no relief from the heat as we separately unloaded our belongings and readied ourselves for our new lives in Carbondale, Illinois. We first met as graduate students, both interested in studying performance at Southern Illinois University (SIU). We both chose SIU having fallen in love with possibilities of performance studies at our subsequent universities: the University of South Florida, where Chris studied with Stacy Holman Jones, Marcy Rose Chvasta, and Elizabeth Bell, and the University of Northern Iowa where Aubrey worked with Karen Mitchell. These women greatly influenced and continue to impact how we conceptualize what it means to perform, teach performance, and commit our work and ourselves to social justice practices.

Our understanding of the connection between performance and social justice strengthened for us while taking classes and developing projects with John Warren, Elyse Pineau, Nathan Stucky, Ron Pelias, Jonny Gray, and Craig Gingrich Philbrook. We were fortunate to take not only classes that included performance methods, theory, and criticism, but also classes in political performance and critical, performance, and communication pedagogies. It was in graduate school that we first became collaborators as teacher–artist–scholars. And, it was in our coursework, which fused social justice, performance, and pedagogy that the burgeoning ideas for this book about creative pedagogical practices as critical acts emerged.

© The Author(s) 2017
C. McRae and A. Huber, *Creating Performances for Teaching and Learning,*
Creativity, Education and the Arts, DOI 10.1007/978-3-319-54561-5_1

1

Over the past 10 years, we have worked together to develop our ideas about critical performance pedagogies. As teachers, we draw from critical, performance, and communication pedagogy scholarship, as well as our experience as performance students, to continuously craft and refine our approach to critical performance pedagogy. We say this to acknowledge that there are many important approaches to critical work and to creative and performance pedagogies. Though our perspective reflects the influences of many others, it is not all encompassing, nor do we mean for it to be. We offer this book as one possibility for engaging in critical performance pedagogy.

We articulate our approach to theorizing and practicing teaching as critical performance pedagogy, which is closely aligned with Pineau's (1994, 1995, 2002) germinal work on critical performative pedagogy. As performance practitioners and scholars, we take seriously Pineau's (1995) call to document and theorize the performance work that we do in our classrooms and pedagogical spaces. We do this as a way to mark what is learned through embodiment and to fully explore and theorize the connections between performance and education.

Pineau (1994) argues that performance has something inherently valuable to add to critical pedagogy research, and "it is a critical moment for performance scholar-practitioners their theoretical and practical knowledge to bear upon this emergent research in education" (p. 5). Teaching as performance is not merely an empty cliché, but functions as powerful metaphor and heuristic that provides careful insights into what it means for bodies to teach and learn. As Pineau articulates, understanding teaching as performance through a performance scholar–practitioner lens "offers a more theoretically sophisticated and methodologically innovative ground for developing new research agendas in educational performance" (p. 5).

For us, theorizing performance and employing performance as a method are essential components of our critical pedagogical approach that strives toward social justice. In defining critical performative pedagogy, Pineau (2002) writes:

> The pedagogy I am advocating embraces performance as a critical methodology that can be fully integrated throughout the learning process. The shift from "body-on-display" to the "body as a medium for learning" requires clarification. In disciplinary terms, performance methodology means rigorous, systematic, exploration-through-enactment of real and imagined experience in which learning occurs through sensory and

kinesthetic engagement (Pineau). In more colloquial terms, performance methodology means learning by doing that might include any experiential approach that asks students to struggle bodily with course content. In addition, performance methodology emphasizes process over product by requiring students to use their bodies systematically over a period of time, rather than simply at the end of the unit. (p. 50)

In other words, critical performative pedagogy requires an intense commitment to embodied learning. Critical performative pedagogy privileges bodies as a medium for learning, focusing corporeal experimentation. Similarly, critical performative pedagogy focuses on process, of bodies becoming, instead of on bodies as finite and finished products.

This embodied, processual approach to learning also emphasizes a pedagogy of social justice. Alexander (2010) extends Pineau's (2002) articulation of critical performative pedagogy, linking it directly to social justice, which he defines by drawing on Madison's (2006) work. He explains:

Social justice is not an end, it is a practice; it is doing. Social justice is a dynamic rehearsal that has no intention of final performance. It is a rehearsal in everyday life toward perfection of social interaction, a process of strategizing the multiple dimensions of being human – being humane, of being in the company of others – that respects the multiple interpretations of that existential human possibility. (p. 333)

Alexander links critical performative pedagogy with social justice in writing: "Critical performative pedagogy is built on the foundations of social justice and must continue to empower students with strategies to critically articulate, translate, and apply such knowledge toward public and social transformation" (p. 334). In other words, critical performative pedagogy engages performance as a way of coming to knowledge *and* as a way of enacting a process of social justice that privileges and strives for inclusivity and equity.

We work to develop, revise, and practice a critical performance pedagogy that works to engage and work toward this articulation of social justice as an ongoing practice. For us, the classroom presents an opportunity for crafting pedagogical approaches that work toward social justice. The micro-practices and mundane communicative acts that take place in the classroom context are all opportunities for moving toward inclusivity, the recognition and respect of others, and reflexive awareness of the ways context enables and constrains certain bodies in ways that are not always symmetrical. In approaching social justice as a process that can be engaged pedagogically, we also work to avoid the pitfall of individualizing the process and accomplishment of social justice. Instead, we emphasize the ways social justice emerges collaboratively, gradually, and over long periods of time. The work of critical performance pedagogy as an enactment of social justice is never complete. Each class, each assignment, and each interaction presents another opportunity for working toward social justice.

Our experience as collaborators and colleagues in performance and pedagogy over the past 10 years has led to numerous projects, discussions, and new ideas about pedagogy, performance, and critical and social justice-oriented scholarship. Over this time, we have created and attempted to create projects that include staged performances, performance workshops, performance assignments, conference presentations, and new courses in communication, performance, and pedagogy. We have also experimented with a variety of performance styles and mediums including playing the trumpet, learning to play the ukulele, making homemade cards, creating stop-motion animation, and writing. One of the consistent themes throughout our collaborative relationship is a focus on how we might engage in performance practices in our teaching and research even when performance might not appear to be the central focus of the classes we are teaching or the research we are engaging. As we begin to interpret and theorize our collaborations, the following questions about pedagogy and performance emerge: How can we bring performance to the classroom (even if the central focus of the class is not necessarily a question of performance)? How can we use performance as a way of developing our pedagogy and research? How might a performance approach transform specific topics or themes? How might performance enable new and different understandings of the world and others? How might performance generate a pedagogy of social justice? How might performance shape the ways we design and conceptualize our classes and assignments? How might both our failed attempts and our successful accomplishments function pedagogically?

What we continue to discover is that performance, as a creative mode of inquiry, always yields new insights. Sometimes these insights are directly related to the questions and problems we are considering. Performance can provide specific answers about teaching and the process of learning. And in other instances performance engenders an indirect solution, or an entirely new line of questioning. Performance may generate new ways of thinking about pedagogy. Either way, performance is a generative mode of inquiry that extends and expands our commitments to critical performance pedagogy and social justice. Performance asks us to attend to the specificity of our practices in the classroom as critical sites of cultural production. Performance asks us to acknowledge the ways our choices as teachers and students constrain and enable our interactions with and amongst others. Performance asks us to develop connections, to listen for context, and to privilege the relationship between bodies and learning.

Throughout this book, we engage and use performance as a means of creating various practices for teaching and learning. This includes the creation of embodied performances, musical practices, practices of crafting, and writing as performance. These practices shape the way we come to think about, make sense of, and develop the philosophy and enactment of our teaching. This book emerges from the realization that our collaborative performance projects present an opportunity for theorizing and engaging in creative practice as acts of critical pedagogy. As you read this book, we invite you, the reader, to collaborate with us in developing this idea of the practice session for pedagogy. We invite you to engage in the consideration and extension of our creative practices as possible sites for extending and expanding your own pedagogical approach. We also invite you to develop and engage your own creative interests, practices, and performances as critical pedagogical acts.

GOALS OF THE BOOK

Our overarching goal in this book is to advocate for the creation of a pedagogy that privileges performance and creative practices as a way to critically work toward social justice. We describe and theorize performance pedagogy as a site for social justice by employing the metaphors of the practice session and the practice space to frame a pedagogy that emphasizes emergent and generative creative practices. The practice session metaphor allows us to consider pedagogical interactions in terms of play, experimentation, repetition, and preparation, articulates a collaborative relationship between teachers and students, and accentuates an embodied approach to learning. Similarly, the practice space metaphor draws attention to the physical limits and possibilities of our pedagogical spaces, highlights the ways in which relationships between teachers and students are constituted, and requires us to examine the implications for educational practices in regard to the stress placed on embodied performances.

This book presents the process and practice of developing performances and other creative projects as the impetus for generating critical philosophies and methods of teaching and learning. In other words, this book presents performance as an embodied tactic for developing and applying critical approaches to pedagogy. Our primary goal is to offer an invitation for students and teachers to create performance as a means for cultivating a philosophy and practice of teaching and learning.

This book works to engage and extend conversations in performance studies, critical pedagogy, and critical communication pedagogy about the relationship between performance and pedagogy by offering an application of performance as a means of generating critical approaches to pedagogy. We emphasize the creative process and practice of developing performance as a generative method and model for creating an approach to teaching and learning that considers creativity and esthetic practices as central to pedagogical efforts that attend to embodiment, diverse perspectives and experiences, and social justice.

This work is applicable to scholars and students with a wide range of interests in education, the classroom, and pedagogy including, but not limited to, communication studies, performance studies, education, and cultural studies. In particular, this book is aimed at expanding conversations about performance and pedagogy in a way that realizes and demonstrates the value of generating performance and creative approaches to education that move beyond the performance classroom. We offer practical suggestions and insights for engaging in performance as a means for generating philosophies and practices of teaching and learning that are grounded in a celebration of the critical implications of creativity and performance.

Throughout the book, we invoke the metaphor of the practice session in order to frame our experience developing performances and artistic/ creative projects. The practice session is a time and space for repetition, refinement, and rehearsal. Practice sessions allow both for the systematic development of performance practices and for experimentation and play in creating new possibilities for performance. The practice session functions as an important moment and method for generating performance, and in this book, the practice session also provides an interpretive framework for theorizing the process of creating performance as an educational and pedagogical act.

The features of the practice session, as a method both for generating performance and for generating pedagogy, are articulated in a presentation and analysis of our own collaborative performance and pedagogical practices. In this book, we present (and perform), our practice of developing various performance projects including staged performance workshops, a project involving the sustained practice of learning and playing musical instruments, a stop-motion video project, and writing workshops. We then theorize the ways these projects shape our philosophies of teaching, the ways we teach students, and the ways our own practices as students are shaped and changed.

By emphasizing the process of developing performances and creative projects, we demonstrate the connection between failure, repetition, and specific moments in rehearsal that lead to insights and new possibilities for our practices as teachers and students. In this book, we theorize the process of creating performance and other artistic and creative projects as a method for developing teaching philosophies and practices of teaching and working with students.

Organization of the Book

In addition to playing with the metaphor of the practice sessions, we use the format of the practice session to structure this text. In Chap. 2, we develop and explain our conceptualizations of the practice session and the practice space, and in the subsequent chapters we offer the examples of practice sessions as a starting place for practitioners to develop their own sessions. Our examples are not meant to be comprehensive, but rather to provide practitioners with a framework for generating creative and collaborative spaces of their own. We have set the book up so that practitioners have the option to use or incorporate the practice sessions we develop here. However, we hope this book will be a springboard for other creative practices and pedagogies and the development of additional practice sessions. Just as we collaborate with one another to develop our ideas, we invite you, the reader, into collaboration with us to generate ideas for additional practice sessions and to further develop possibilities for critical performance pedagogy.

In the spirit of pedagogical collaboration, we present and structure each of the chapters in this book using the format of a lesson plan. Our ideas are organized in the same ways we often organize or plan lessons in a classroom context. We offer this structure with two goals in mind. First, the lesson plan is a way for us to organize, present, and enact our ideas and pedagogy. If this book is a pedagogical practice session, then the chapter of the book functions as the space for us to present and share our lessons. The second goal of using the lesson plan as an organizing structure is to frame our ideas within, what we hope, is the invitational structure of a pedagogical context. These lesson plans, and chapters, are offered as pedagogical moments and openings for you to consider, to extend, and to transform.

Each chapter begins with an agenda as a form of previewing the specific goals for each of our lessons/chapters. We then offer a warm-up in each chapter as a way to develop awareness, focus, and preparation for the discussions and themes in each chapter. These warm-up activities are not unlike the warm-up activities we use in our own communication and performance classes. They are descriptive invitations of sensory engagements that are designed to frame the content of each lesson, emphasize the role of the body as a site of learning and knowledge production, and to exemplify and model a possible pedagogical strategy for future use. After each warm-up activity, we debrief the engagement in order to draw attention to pedagogical and theoretical implications that are related to the specific theme of each chapter.

In the sections following the discussion of the warm-up activity, we present the themes of each chapter regarding the pedagogical and critical significance of performance and creative practices including staged performance, music, crafting, and writing. The goal of articulating these thematic sections is to provide a theoretical foundation for developing performance practices that are pedagogically relevant and critically driven. In these sections, we offer our own performance and creative practices as possible examples for future classroom practices.

Each chapter or lesson also includes an engagement that outlines possible strategies for applying, extending, and working with the creative practices presented in each chapter. The engagements are set up much like the warm-up activities in that they are written as suggestions for/ directions to practitioners. The idea behind the engagements is to offer you with a practical activity that you could use, or adapt and use, in your own classrooms or pedagogical spaces.

We end each chapter in a way similar to the way we end our own classes: with a brief closing section to synthesize and summarize ideas from the chapter. Just as we try to wrap up lessons in our classes by tracking important themes and noting limitations, we also try to review relevant ideas for the reader. We provide these summaries in an effort to transparent about how we are tying things together, and to provide an additional model of our approach to pedagogy. This same lesson plan structure is used throughout each of the chapters. In the following paragraphs, we briefly discuss the specific focus of each chapter.

In Chap. 2, "Practice Space," we introduce and define the metaphors of the practice space and practice session as the guiding frame for the arguments presented throughout this book about the relationship between creative practices and critical pedagogy. The practice session suggests a time and place for initiating a sustained process of experimentation, repetition, and refinement of acts and ideas. The practice session also functions as a metaphor that is, for us, productively linked to theories of performance studies that understand performance as a creative and culturally situated act. In other words, the practice session is an act of performance that works to imagine and make realities.

The practice *space* is the location of the practice session. Physically, the practice space is a unique location that allows and even encourages creative and generative practices. In this chapter, we define the practice space as a physical and a theoretical location. Physically, we articulate and define our book as a kind of practice space, or location, for experimenting with and rehearsing ideas about the relationship between performance and critical pedagogy. Theoretically, we locate our project within the research contexts of performance studies, critical pedagogy, and critical communication pedagogy. We call for the recognition and development of physical and theoretical spaces for practice in terms of the creation of embodied and inclusive pedagogies. We imagine the classroom as a practice space, and the interactions and events that take place in the classroom as creative and generative acts of practice and rehearsal.

In Chap. 3, "Performance as Research," we describe the first of our five practice sessions. This first practice session focuses on the practice of the performance workshop. In this chapter, we specifically feature performance as a way of conducting and staging research questions. We contend that performance workshops provide the space for generating new insights about and possibilities for human interaction and communication. We begin by articulating three characteristics of performance workshops. First, performance workshops emphasize embodiment and experimentation. Second, performance workshops offer space to generate new perspectives. Third, performance workshops prioritize interaction amongst participants and therefore function as exercise in community building.

We then discuss how performance workshops can function as acts of research, connection across difference, and transformation. We specifically forward the argument for performance as way to administer research and

to stage research questions. We also focus on the ways performance provides the space for creating and sharing understandings across difference.
Finally, as an act of critical pedagogy, the performance workshop also functions to develop an awareness of the status quo and provides the opportunity to imagine possibilities for change. Throughout this chapter, we
theorize the ways performance workshops function as a creative practice
for teaching and learning in the service of social justice. We also provide
several possible workshop prompts and ideas for engaging in performance
as a way of extending and expanding various research questions.

In Chap. 4, "Music and Routine," we present the musical practice session
as a creative process that reveals insights about the function of routines and
experimentation. This chapter offers an extended discussion of specific musical practices as generative forms of inquiry that can be used to extend critical approaches to pedagogy. Working from the example of our experiences
learning and playing musical instruments, we use the context of our musical
practice in order to develop and extend our arguments about the pedagogical and political functions of creativity. Musical experience or skill is not necessary for an appreciation or application of this session. Rather, this practice
session opens the space for the recognition of how the design of routine and
experimentation can work to critically recognize and engage larger structures
especially in pedagogical contexts. We argue music making can function as
critical pedagogy in that it is culturally located and enacted on and by bodies
(McRae 2015, pp. 4–5) and therefore has the potential to highlight specific
ways that cultural practices are (re)constituted by both musicians and audiences. As a creative act, music making can be further understood as critical
pedagogy in that it is a site of embodied inquiry into the production of not
only individual, but cultural, and social performances.

In addition to arguing for music making as critical pedagogy, we contend that making music emphasizes the cultivation of routine, which is
necessary for understanding and facilitating critical pedagogy. For instance,
routines function to organize and bodies. In organizing bodies, routines
discipline bodies into particular practices, which may maintain social ideological structures. On the other hand, routines can also be developed to
generate new practices that might subvert and resist the status quo. To
illustrate how music routines are developed, we describe the process of one
of the authors continued practice of over 20 years of playing the trumpet,
and of the other author's learning to play the ukulele. These musical practices offer an example of the pedagogical implications of the performances
of learning through routine and experimentation.

Chapter 5, "Crafting Pictures and Reflexivity," focuses on the pedagogical function of creative practices and performances of crafting. The practice space for crafting and handmade art offers a metaphor for thinking through the ways artful and creative practices enable new ways of reflexively and critically thinking about, understanding, and making sense of the world and our interactions with others. We discuss the practice of card-making and our collaborative process of developing a stop-motion animation video. The process of creating handmade cards and stop-motion animation offer insights regarding the development of creative and critical pedagogies. In this chapter, we describe the challenges and questions that emerge during our crafting practices as examples of the kinds of questions and reflexive process that become possible in the practice space of sustained crafting and handmade art practices. We end this chapter with an invitation for engagement with an artistic practice session as a generative approach to refining and critically thinking about classroom practices, pedagogical interaction, and processes of learning.

In Chap. 6, we present and consider the performance of writing as a creative pedagogical practice that can work toward moments of social justice. Using the language of performance, we discuss the pedagogical value of writing for experimentation, rehearsal, and enactment of new ideas. Performance functions as a framework for interrogating the possibilities of writing as a creative and generative pedagogical practice. A sustained writing routine is not only a practice of cultivating ideas; it is also an embodied act of training the body to perform on the page. The habit of writing invites us to slow down, reflect back upon, and examine concrete experiences in ways that reveal patterns of our existence. Working from our own pedagogical use of daily writing journals and our experience writing in collaboration, we also consider the ways writing might be used to experiment and imagine new and better ways of being in the world.

In Chap. 7, "Future Sessions," we emphasize the importance of recognizing the value of creative practices as essential for working toward social justice. We invite future sessions that articulate creative practices that exemplify and extend the connections between art and social justice. As an invitation to begin crafting future sessions, we offer several examples of everyday creative practices, which may be cultivated to generate possibilities for social justice work. In this chapter, we call for the creation of pedagogical approaches that invite imagination, creativity, process, and the room for failure. Finally, we make the case for future sessions that continue to revise, reinvent, and re-envision the practice session as a space for engaging creativity, critical pedagogy, and social justice.

A PRACTICE SESSION FOR PEDAGOGY

The classroom is a site full of possibilities for new understandings, experimentation, and emerging relationships. As teachers invested in the study of performance and communication, we approach the classroom as a location where research and teaching are intertwined, where theory and practice are inseparable, and where consequential realities are made in and through the daily interactions and performances of the classroom.

Our approach to the classroom informs the ways we theorize and enact pedagogy throughout this book in terms of the metaphor of the practice session. The classroom is a site for developing, maintaining, and transforming various practices. Each chapter of this book centers on specific pedagogical practices and creative acts. However, our hope is that the individual chapters of this book function together to create an overall practice session for pedagogy as a creative and critical act. In other words, we hope that this book works to create a space and a structure for practicing, theorizing, and engaging in creative and critical approaches to teaching and learning.

For us, one of the most important features of the classroom, and of the practice of teaching, is the relationships that emerge between and amongst students and teachers. These relationships present possibilities for the creation of new and transformative ideas. And one of our biggest hopes in writing this book is that we might engage you in a pedagogical relationship that is invitational and generative. We offer this practice session for pedagogy as one possibility for developing philosophies and practices of teaching that are grounded in esthetic, creative, and critical approaches to education. We offer each of the chapters as lesson plans in order to invite your consideration and contribution. These lesson plans are suggestions, they are options, and they are dynamic frameworks for future work. We encourage you to extend these ideas, challenge our approaches, and transform these lesson plans through your own creative and critical work as teachers and students.

REFERENCES

Alexander, B. K. (2010). Critical/performative/pedagogy: Performing possibility as a rehearsal for social justice. In D. L. Fassett & J. T. Warren (Eds.), *The Sage handbook of communication and instruction* (pp. 315–342). Thousand Oaks, CA: Sage.

Madison, D. S. (2006). Staging fieldwork/performing human rights. In D. S. Madison & J. Hamera (Eds.), *The Sage handbook of performance studies* (pp. 397–418). Thousand Oaks, CA: Sage.

McRae, C. (2015). Hearing performance as music. *Liminalities: A Journal of Performance Studies, 11*(5), 1–19.

Pineau, E. L. (1994). Teaching is performance: Reconceptualizing a problematic metaphor. *American Educational Research Journal, 31*(1), 3–25.

Pineau, E. L. (1995). Re-casting rehearsal: Making a case for production as research. *Journal of the Illinois Speech and Theatre Association, 46,* 43–52.

Pineau, E. L. (2002). Critical performative pedagogy: Fleshing out the politics of liberatory education. In N. Stucky & C. Wimmer (Eds.), *Teaching performance studies* (pp. 41–54). Carbondale, IL: Southern Illinois University Press.

CHAPTER 2

Practice Space

In this chapter, we introduce and define the metaphors of the practice space and practice session as the guiding frame for the arguments presented throughout this book about the relationship between creative practices and critical pedagogy. In particular, the practice session suggests a time and place for initiating a sustained process of experimentation, repetition, and refinement of acts and ideas. The practice session also functions as a metaphor that is, for us, productively linked to theories of performance studies that understand performance as a creative and culturally situated act. In other words, the practice session is an act of performance that works to imagine and make realities.

The practice *space* is the location of the practice session. Physically, the practice space is a unique location that allows and even encourages creative and generative practices. In this chapter, we define the practice space as a physical and a theoretical location. Physically, we articulate and define our book as a kind of practice space, or location, for experimenting with and rehearsing ideas about the relationship between performance and critical pedagogy. Theoretically, we locate our project within the research contexts of performance studies, critical pedagogy, and critical communication pedagogy (CCP). We call for the recognition and development of physical and theoretical spaces for practice in terms of the creation of embodied and inclusive pedagogies. We imagine the classroom as a practice space, and the interactions and events that take place in the classroom as creative and generative acts of practice and rehearsal.

© The Author(s) 2017   15
C. McRae and A. Huber, *Creating Performances for Teaching and Learning*,
Creativity, Education and the Arts, DOI 10.1007/978-3-319-54561-5_2

Agenda

1. Warm-up
2. Creative practices and critical pedagogy
3. Defining practice sessions and spaces
4. Engagement: Creating classroom practice spaces and sessions
5. Closing

WARM-UP
Sensory Focus

Take a deep breath.
Exhale.
(*Repeat*)
Notice the way the space feels around you.
What is the temperature in the space where you are reading? Is it hot? Is it cold? Is it humid? Is it dry? Is there snow? Or, is there ice? Is there fog? How does your skin feel? Are you dry? Are you sweating? Do you feel a chill? Is your body tense? Is your body relaxed?
Notice the textures of the space. Do you feel the bumpiness of a plastic classroom chair or some other surface? Do you feel the smooth wood casing of the pencil you're using to make notes in the margins? Do you feel the rough uneven texture of plaster walls? Do you feel the cool terrazzo tile, or fuzzy carpet, or smooth wood, underneath your bare feet? How is your body interacting with or relating to the space?
Notice the physical limits of the space.
How does the space enable you to read? Are you sitting? Standing? Crouching? Leaning? Hunching? Laying down? On the move? What is the size of the space? How are you contained within it? What other objects or people inhabit the space with you? Are you in a library? Are you at a table in your favorite restaurant? Snuggled up in your favorite chair at home? Uncomfortably squeezed into the middle seat of an airplane? Are you wandering around a park or garden? Or, riding an empty metro?
Take a deep breath.
Exhale.
Notice the sounds in the space around you.
Is there music? Are there conversations? Are there humming lights or appliances? Is there a phone ringing? Do you hear other bodies moving

around you? Are there dogs, or cats, or birds? Is there a baby crying or child vying for attention? Can you hear the wind? Running water? The whir of a mountain breeze? Do you hear sirens? Is there traffic? Do you hear the sounds of construction?

Notice the sounds of your body.

Listen to the sound of your breathing. Hear the sound of your voice as you softly read these words out loud.

Take a deep breath.

Exhale.

Notice the scents and odors of the space around you.

Are there pleasant fragrances and aromas? Is there a freshly brewed pot of coffee? Or, is there a vegetable curry simmering on the stove? Are there cookies in the oven? Is there a lingering smell of cologne or lotion? Do you smell freshly cut grass? Or newly fallen leaves? Do you smell rain? Is there a foul stench in the air? Do you smell burnt toast? Or the chemical scent of cleaner? Do you smell cigarette smoke? Or the sweet smell of pipe tobacco? Do you smell exhaust from a car? Or a nearby factory? Smell the pages of this book. Does it smell inky, fresh off the presses? Musty? Does it smell like the tea you spilled on it this morning?

Take a deep breath.

Exhale.

Notice the flavor of the space around you.

Taste the air in the space as you inhale. Do you taste rain? Is there water in the air in the form of fog, mist, or snow? Take a swig of the beverage you've been sipping. What is the flavor of your drink? Coffee? Tea? Fruit/Vegetable Juice? Lemonade? Smoothie? Milkshake? Powdered Supplement? Wine? Beer? Water? How does the city, spring, river, well, or purified water taste? Is there a lingering taste in your mouth from your last meal or snack? Or the minty flavor of mouthwash or toothpaste? Or the acridity of a sour grape?

Take a deep breath.

Exhale.

Notice the sights of the space around you.

Is the light bright from an overhead fixture or large window? Is the light of the sun shining on you? Is there a glare? Is there a soft glow from a lamp or a flickering candle? Are there shadows from the trees or clouds? What catches the corner of your eye? Do you see the subtle movement from another body? Can you see the color of your shirt? Or do you see the beckoning light from your phone or computer? Are there people in your midst? Notice the color of the pages of this book. How do they stand in contrast to the lights and colors of the space around you?

Take a deep breath.

Exhale.

Debriefing the Warm-up

We imagine that you, the reader, may engage with some of the prompts and provocations of our sensory focus activity. We hope you tried some of this exercise because we want you to begin thinking about and *noticing* the space around you, and your relationship to and with that space. Pedagogically, warming-up offers a starting place and a way to begin developing focus and attention to particular themes, ideas, and contexts. Warming-up also privileges the body, and embodied ways of knowing and theorizing. For us, warming-up is a way of preparing our bodies to engage with and generate ideas. And this warm-up, in particular, is a way of preparing for our discussion about practice sessions and spaces. This activity also features our commitment to performance and performance studies research in educational contexts.

Warming-up with Performance

In performance studies research, the recognition of the classroom space and the act of teaching as transformational is not a new argument. For example, Stucky and Wimmer (2002) contend: "The classroom is a charged space, a site of performance as well as a place invested in studying performances. Teachers have increasingly come to understand the special characteristics of classrooms as environments where performance holds particular power" (p. 2). The power of performance in the classroom is also noted by Pineau (1994) in her re-conceptualization of the metaphor of teaching as performance. She explains:

> The critical question is not whether teaching is or is not a performance. Educational and theatrical stages are not identical, and the aesthetic responsibilities and conventions of the educational performer are not the same as those that govern stage performers. Rather, the inclusionary impulse in performance studies allows us to ask in what ways educational phenomena open themselves up to performance-centered research. How

might the disciplinary knowledge of performance studies enrich pedagogical uses of performance as both metaphor and methodology? (p. 9)

In other words, performance offers a way of transforming and expanding educational spaces and practices that exceeds reductive extensions and applications of theatrical objectives and practices to educational interactions. Throughout this book, we extend the commitments of performance studies research to an embodiment, critical engagement/analysis, and generative practices specifically to the development of a pedagogy that features the space and time for creative practices as a critical imperative.

The warm-up activity at the beginning of this chapter is informed by our commitment to generating a pedagogy that emphasizes embodiment and that recognizes the classroom as a site for working toward and enacting social change. Boal's (1979) call for a theater and poetics of the oppressed presents an ethic that informs our approach to performance, and to the development of embodied engagements in the classroom space such as our warm-up activity. Boal's goal for transforming the space of theater is a goal that resonates with our commitment to the classroom space. He explains:

> But the *poetics of the oppressed* focuses on the action itself: the spectator delegates no power to the character (or actor) either to act or to think in his place; on the contrary, he himself assumes the protagonic role, changes the dramatic action, tries out solutions, discusses plans for change—in short, trains himself for real action. In this case, perhaps the theatre is not revolutionary in itself, but it is surely a rehearsal for the revolution. The liberated spectator, as a whole person, launches into action. No matter that the action is fictional; what matters is that it is action! (p. 98)

For Boal, the theater presents an important space and opportunity for imagining new possibilities for social interactions and relationships. He imagines and works to maintain a theatrical space, without passive spectators. Audience members are, for Boal, potential agents of change, and theater is a space for rehearsing and creating possibilities for liberation. By extending this specification of theater to the classroom space, Boal's ideas provide a framework for engaging students as active participants in working toward change. Boal emphasizes the body, and an awareness of embodiment, as a central aspect of re-imaging the theater as a liberatory space:

We can begin by stating that the first word of the theatrical vocabulary is the human body, the main source of sound and movement. Therefore, to control the means of theatrical production, man must, first of all, control his own body, know his own body, in order to be capable of making it more expressive. Then he will be able to practice theatrical forms in which by stages he frees himself from his condition of spectator and takes on that of actor, in which he ceases to be an object and becomes a subject, is changed from witness into protagonist. (p. 102)

By developing an awareness of the expressive potential of the body, spectators-turned-performers can begin to realize the ways theater may be deployed and engaged as a rehearsal space for social change. Understanding the specificity and potential of the body is a key to marking the shift from a passive audience of spectators to an engaged and active body of performers. In the classroom context, this cultivation of bodily awareness is similarly central to imaging the classroom as a space for creating and enacting change.

One way of drawing attention to our embodied experience is by developing our sensory focus on the ways our bodies function in relationship to and with the spaces we inhabit. As Pineau (1995) explains:

Since performance is a methodology of enactment, a learning by doing, it must proceed through direct kinesthetic engagement with the issues to be explored. Performing bodies function as the vehicle for asking research questions and they become the means of data collection, for they are the site at which the data presents itself to the researcher. (p. 48)

Therefore, the warm-up offered at the beginning of this chapter is one example and possibility for raising questions about the relationship between bodies and pedagogical spaces. By drawing attention to the sensory and sensual experiences of our bodies, we offer a starting place for theorizing and realizing the ways our bodies are always interconnected with the spaces where we learn and interact with each other. The guiding prompts in our warm-up are aimed at foregrounding how: "In the classroom, the body serves not only as a performing ideologically saturated cultural being, but also as an enfleshed being situated in education—as a body that is capable of learning viscerally" (Warren 1999, p. 258).

Warming-up the Senses: Absences and Presences

The prompts offered in the warm-up follow the work of Stewart (2011) who proposes "atmospheric attunement" as a process of attending to and pausing to note the ways the world emerges around us. She explains this as:

An attention to the matterings, the complex emergent worlds, happening in everyday life. The rhythms of living that are addictive or shifting. The kinds of agency that might or might not add up to something with some kind of intensity or duration. The enigmas and oblique events and background noises that might be barely sensed and yet are compelling. (p. 445)

This process of engaging the mundane happenings of the world as they emerge, and come to matter, in sensory ways begins to reveal connections and points of contact we share with our world. For example, the sensory cues that are (or are not) available to us through touch, sound, smell, taste, or sight begin to demonstrate the ways we are culturally and individually located in the world. Our privileges, desires, possibilities, and constraints are embedded and revealed in the visceral and everyday phenomena that our bodies contact.

Attending to sensory experience is often characterized by an attention to taken-for-granted aspects of our everyday experiences. Leder's (1990) phenomenological work demonstrates the ways the body, and technologies of the body, become absent or disappear (p. 35). Westerkamp's (1974) call for soundwalking and "uncompromised listening" is an approach that attempts to highlight the otherwise taken-for-granted sounds of our environment (p. 18). Similarly, Henshaw's (2013) extension of soundwalking to olfactory experiences of urban spaces through smellwalks offers an example of the ways attention to particular sensory experiences might inform and shape the ways spaces are understood and engaged.

Attending to the taken-for-granted sensory characteristics of the environment is a practice that can revitalize a sensory understanding of the world. The five senses offer a guiding framework for recognizing and organizing the characteristics of the world (smells, sounds, sights, tastes, and tactile aspects) that might otherwise seem to disappear or become absent. However, the goal of this activity is not to simply catalog the perception of our discrete senses. This engagement also works to center our attention on the role our body plays in the experience of the world and of making the world present and knowable.

For example, in her consideration of the installation performance work and audio walks of artist Janet Cadiff, Féral (2012) considers the relationship between perception and presence effects. Cadiff's work creates aural experiences and situations for audience members through recordings that either match existing locations or fabricated installations. Féral explains, "Cardiff creates sound effects that give the spectator the impression that he or she is elsewhere, in a real space surrounded by others, though the spectator knows that he or she is in reality alone" (p. 39). For Féral, these installations work to experiment with and highlight the significance of perception and the body in the production of presence effects through what she refers to as a "carnal coefficient" (p. 44). She explains:

> In every "presence effect" on the spectator, there is a carnal coefficient brought into play. The body is interpellated by way of the sensory organs (eye, ear), and also by the spectator's sensations, a body which is simultaneously an essential element and an obstacle because it has some opacity. (p. 44)

Sensory perception functions as a necessary multiplier in the production of presence effects. For Féral, presence effects are therefore always a sensed experience; however, these effects are also always mediated by the body. The carnal coefficient is a critical part of the equation in the production of presence effects, and it is also a way of understanding the sensory functions of the body as operating in ways that are interrelated and connected rather than as a set of five discrete sensory tools.

In our warm-up activity, the five senses are engaged in order to both notice aspects of the world that often go unnoticed or are otherwise absent, and to draw attention to the ways bodies make the world present. The carnal coefficient of the body constitutes experiences that are always located in social and cultural spaces. Attending in specific and guided ways to the sensory experience of the world provides an opening for identifying the ways the body always shapes and constitutes the world around us. In the space of the classroom, this activity functions as a way of centering on the body as central to the process of teaching and learning. Not only are bodies often taken-for-granted in educational spaces, but bodies also constitute what is knowable and what may become knowable in educational contexts.

CREATIVE PRACTICES AND CRITICAL PEDAGOGY

The metaphors of the practice session and practice space offer a productive starting place for theorizing and enacting creative pedagogical practices. Practice sessions are events for learning, and practice spaces are locations for learning. These metaphors, and this overall project, are informed by work in performance studies, creative pedagogy, critical pedagogy, and CCP. For us, the creative and performative practices that emerge in practice sessions and spaces are practices that can also work toward enacting and realizing the social justice goals of critical pedagogy.

Connecting to Performance Studies

Our work in pedagogy is informed by the research and theoretical perspectives of performance studies. Performance is, for us, both an object of study *and* the primary subject of the classes we teach (Conquergood 1983; Pelias and Van Oosting 1987). To be more specific, performance offers a means of explaining and understanding human communication as an embodied, constitutive, and generative process. Hamera's (2006) definition of performance indicates the significance of performance for our work as teachers and researchers. She explains:

> Performance is both an event and a heuristic tool that illuminates the presentational and representational elements of culture. Its inherent 'eventness' ('in motion') makes it especially effective for engaging and describing the embodied processes that produce and consume culture. As event or as heuristic, performance makes thing and does things, in addition to describing how they are made or done. (p. 6)

Performance offers a productive site of study (performed events, actions, etc.), and it offers a way of explaining and theorizing human interactions as shaped by and generative of cultural forms and formations. Finally, performance offers a strategy for imagining and enacting new and different cultural practices.

In educational and classroom contexts, performance presents a particularly useful model for theorizing learning as an embodied, cultural and critical act (Dolan 1996; Pineau 1994). Performance attends to learning, and ways of knowing, that emerge from the culturally located site of the body (Taylor 2003, p. 3). In other words, a performance studies approach raises questions about how we come to know through our bodies; how our embodied learning and knowing works to enact various cultural formations. For example, Butler's (1988) discussion of gender as a performative accomplishment indicates the interrelated relationship between bodies and culture (p. 523). For Butler, gender is constituted in and through the repetitions of performances that "render(s) social laws explicit" (p. 526). In this way, performance is a critical site of learning about and producing cultural forms of knowledge that carry material consequences.

Performance also offers the potential for the creation of critical and generative responses in educational contexts. Conquergood (2002) explains performance studies can be characterized by a commitment to "creativity, critique, citizenship (civic struggles for social justice)" (p. 152). These commitments inform our use of performance in educational contexts as a method. In other words, we work to recognize learning as embodied and accomplished in performance, but we are also committed to developing new ways of performing, knowing, and enacting culture in our educational practice. In the following section, we discuss the application of performance in educational contexts as a creative and generative practice.

Performance as Creative Pedagogy

Performance studies features methods that generate staged performance work and aesthetic presentations (Pelias 2014, pp. 133–134). These often creative, imaginative, and artistic methods of performance can offer important insights about pedagogical practices, and these methods are also closely related to the goals of a broader sense of creativity in education. Eisner's (2004) argument about the transformative contribution of the arts to the practice of education is similar to the kinds of possibilities performance methods offer education. In terms of the possibilities engendered by an arts-based approach to pedagogy, Eisner maintains:

At the risk of propagating dualisms, but in the service of emphasis, I am talking about a culture of schooling in which more importance is placed on exploration than on discovery, more value is assigned to surprise than to control, more attention is devoted to what is distinctive than to what is standard, more interest is related to what is metaphorical than to what is literal. (p. 10)

Likewise, performance methods in pedagogical contexts (both in the creation of classroom practices and in generating theoretical approaches to teaching) work to privilege discovery, disruption, and emergent ideas.

Pineau's (1994) organizational strategy for articulating the relationship between performance and education in terms of educational poetics, play, process, and power reveals some of the transformative ways performance studies might be used to engage educational contexts. Each of these four categories offers a starting place for our thinking about the relationship between performance studies and pedagogy, and more broadly between performance and creativity in educational contexts.

Pineau (1994) first offers a definition of educational poetics that is characterized by an emphasis on the aesthetic dimensions of teaching and learning, and by attention to the multiple narratives, metaphors, and performances that constitute educational interactions (pp. 10–13). Educational poetics attends to the structures, languages, and practices that constitute educational practices and spaces. The second category Pineau presents as a link between performance and pedagogy is educational play. Play, in and through performance, enables a pedagogy that features improvisation, experimentation, and disruption of taken-for-granted educational and instructional practices (pp. 13–15). The third category Pineau offers is an educational process. In terms of performance, educational process emphasizes performance as a method and process of generating understanding and knowledge in the classroom space (pp. 15–18). Finally, Pineau describes educational power as a way that performance research might be used to develop and enact critiques of educational practices and assumption (pp. 18–21). These four categories offer a starting place for using performance in educational research and for developing pedagogical approaches that emphasize embodied and creative ways of learning and teaching.

The categories of educational poetics, play, process, and power also point to the ways performance can offer a systematic approach to shaping a creative educational practice. Performance can yield a generative and creative pedagogy, but its performance is also a rigorous endeavor. Finally, it is important to note that our approach to performance as a creative educational practice works to build on the call for creativity in education that is not driven by the goals of standardization and marketability. Rather we are invested in what Harris (2014) refers to as a "process-focused creativity (p. 20). The creativity that performance strives to introduce in educational contexts embraces process, critique, and the productive possibilities of failure (Harris 2014, pp. 20–28). In the following section, we discuss the ways critical pedagogy, CCP, and the goals of social justice education inform our pedagogical commitment to performance.

Connecting to Critical Pedagogy

Critical pedagogy is founded in the writing and teaching of Brazilian literacy educator, Paulo Freire. Freire's (1970/2000) germinal work, *Pedagogy of the Oppressed*, locates injustice(s) as constituted in the reciprocal relationship of oppressor and oppressed. Put simply, the oppressor emerges as s/he accumulates and possesses goods, capital, and therefore power whereas the oppressed is dependent on, underneath, and subservient to the oppressor (p. 64). This system persists over time as new groups of people learn and are educated into their position(s) in the world. The oppressed and oppressor alike internalize this caste system with an elite class and working class. Oppressors work to maintain this system through various mechanisms of dehumanization and what Freire calls, "false generosity" or "false charity," in which oppressors express benevolence toward the oppressed while the status quo remains intact (pp. 44–45). Freire advocates a pedagogy of the oppressed, in which the oppressed, through a critical consciousness, "*conscientizção*," become aware of the mechanisms that oppress them and develop strategies for taking action to liberate themselves (p. 34).

Though Freire's program was developed to teach literacy to the Brazilian working class to empower them with the tools and strategies to understand the dominating devices of their government, his work has been extended to educative contexts. Similar to the way the oppressed are educated to inhabit particular statuses, students are also schooled in ways that reproduce particular inequalities. This work has been developed into what is now recognized as critical pedagogy, in which educators, in conjunction with students, work to reveal systemic inequality and strategize solutions that are in line with social justice. Kincheloe (2008) summarizes this idea in his primer on critical pedagogy:

> Any viable vision of critical education has to be based on larger social and cognitive visions. In this context, educators deal not only with questions of schooling, curriculum, and educational policy but also with social justice and human possibility. Understanding these dynamics, critical educators devise new modes of making connections between school and its context as well as catalyzing community resources to help facilitate quality education with an impassioned spirit. With this larger vision in mind and knowledge of these different contexts, educate are empowered to identify the insidious forces that subvert particular students. (p. 7)

Unlike traditional educational methods, critical pedagogy asks educators and students to work together to examine the mechanisms of education and how they function to produce and reproduce larger systems of power, privilege, and access. Ethnographic studies of classroom environments support the development of the body of critical pedagogy research. Notable examples include Willis's (1981) study of British boys schools producing and reproducing a working class, McLaren's (1986/1999) study of cultural ritual in schools, Warren's (2003) critical ethnography of race and performance, Grande's (2004) example of American Indian education, and Pascoe's (2007) study of sexuality and masculinity in schools.

Connecting to Critical Communication Pedagogy

CCP practitioners and scholars have contributed to developed critical pedagogy to include an examination of the ways in which communication constitutes classrooms, students, teachers, learning, and education in particular ways that often reify social hierarchies and systemic inequities. In line with critical pedagogy, Fassett and Warren (2006) describe 10 commitments to frame CCP and distinguish it from critical pedagogy. These commitments include: understanding identity is constituted in communication; understanding power as fluid and complex; understanding of culture as complex and a central component of communication, as opposed to something that is added on; focusing concrete, mundane communication practices to reveal how they are constitutive of larger social structural systems; embracing social structural critique(s) to situate mundane communication practices; understanding language as constitutive of lived realities; emphasizing pedagogy and research as praxis; developing a complex and nuanced understating of human subjectivity and agency (with students, research participants, co-investigators, etc.); and finally, engaging in dialogue as a metaphor and method for understanding and engaging in relationships (pp. 39–54). In summarizing CCP, Cooks (2010) writes:

> CCP places communication as central to any understanding of what it is that we do when we teach and when we learn. That is our expectations of what should take place in any instructional context are created in and through communication. (p. 303)

Cooks further describes how CCP's contribution is unique and enhances what is already happening in critical pedagogy research: "In CCP, both formal and mundane practices become the focus of study and attention: How do teachers and students make sense of what is largely unremarkable, as well as those moments in which something occurs to break the routine?" (p. 304). In other words, CCP scholars maintain commitments and practices of critical pedagogy research and further cultivate it through particular attention to micro-moments of communicative phenomena.

Similarly, CCP scholars often cultivate their research using ethnographic methods. CCP scholars also embrace autoethnographic methods in order to draw attention to communicative productions of identity (class, race, gender, ability, sexuality, etc.) and the ways in which power, privilege, and access affect these productions. Alexander's (2011) explanation of autography helps to frame the role of autoethnography in CCP:

> Autoethnography is always about cultures of experience: the presenter uses individual experience as a means of engaging in a public discussion or discourse of the particular happenstance of experience, and others are always interpolated into that experience; either for immediate conversation or reflective engagement on their own processes of sense making. Autoethnography draws on Geertz's (1973) extension of thick description as a means of describing and embodying behaviors, giving the audience an experiential instance for understanding the meaningfulness of expression, and the political importance of the utterance in a larger cultural context. (p. 100)

Gathering and developing a thick description of classroom contexts using ethnographic and autoethnographic methods, CCP scholars can pinpoint how local examples of inequality are directly connected to larger global and social structures of power, privilege, and access.

Enacting Social Justice

While a key element of critical pedagogy is to reveal inequality and the ways in which inequality is maintained and perpetuated, the underlying goal is, as Kincheloe suggests, finding ways to enact social justice. Similarly, CCP scholars cite social justice as the ultimate goal of their teaching and research. Warren and Fassett (2010) argue:

> Critical communication pedagogy increases attention to issues of social justice as a fundamental and integral part of our work as researchers and teachers of communication. Too often, the rhetoric that surrounds being in academic life invites us to rest comfortably in unquestioned assumptions, for example, that knowledge is valuable for its own sake or that education is inevitably competitive; however, the critical tradition calls such beliefs into question, asking instead how such knowledge works in the world and for whom such knowledge is produced. (p. 289)

As the keystone of critical pedagogy and CCP research and practice, social justice is central to the way we understand and advocate for creativity to the classroom.

To situate social justice, we draw on Sensoy and DiAngelo's (2012) explanation of "critical social justice." This approach:

> recognizes that society is stratified (i.e., divided and unequal) in significant and far-reaching ways along social group lines that include race, class, gender, sexuality, and ability. Critical social justice recognizes inequality as deeply embedded in the fabric of society (i.e., as structural), and actively seeks to change this. (p. xviii).

Understanding social stratification and wanting to find ways of changing inequality, it is also important to be able to envision what it might mean to realize social justice and live in a just world. In her review of social justice in education, Hytten (2006) describes and defines the tenets of such an environment:

In a just society, there is an equitable distribution of resources, goods, services and opportunities. People are treated as ends in themselves, with the ability to determine their own life goals in interdependent relationship with people around them. They are not used for other people's benefit. (p. 223)

In other words, this approach to social justice in education includes understanding how education functions to stratify individuals in particular ways and tries to find equitable ways to provide access to goods, services, and opportunities in order to undo mechanisms of dehumanization. For us, recognizing inequity and enacting social justice can be accomplished by generating opportunities for students to engage in performance and creativity in the classroom.

Enacting Critical Performative Pedagogy

Just as CCP emphasizes how specific communicative practices constitute the ways bodies are schooled, disciplined, and educated, in order to open up and reveal opportunities for social justice, performance can draw attention to these micro-moments, and through performance, we can begin to imagine and enact change. Building from critical pedagogy and alongside CCP, we align ourselves with what Pineau (2002) has called a "critical performative pedagogy," in which practitioners and scholars draw on the body and embodied performance to reveal and theorize how social structures are created, maintained, and changed in and through performance. She situates the agenda for critical performative pedagogy within three dimensions. First, critical performative pedagogy acknowledges:

inequities in power and privilege have physical impact on bodies and consequently must be struggled against bodily, through physical action and activism. Critical performative pedagogy puts bodies into action in the classroom because it believes this is the surest way to become alive in the social sphere. (p. 53)

This is to say that social inequity manifests on and in bodies. To engage such pressures and structures, bodies act; they must perform.

Second, Pineau explains critical performative pedagogy's commitment to cultivating research that "accounts for how particular bodies present themselves in the classroom and provide detailed and evocative accounts of what one *sees* and *experiences* in the course of a study" (p. 53). It is important to document (write and perform) the specific instances that bodies are affected by power structures. Pineau argues for performance as a way to reveal the embodied implications of and for social ideologies.

Finally, Pineau describes how critical performative pedagogy strategizes ways to extend performance methodologies into contexts beyond the performance classroom. She contends that by employing performance, within a wide array of contexts, students, practitioners, and researchers will gain insights into the ways in which reality is constituted through embodied performance, and how it can be changed in and through bodies.

Drawing from performance studies, critical pedagogy, CCP, and framing our work in critical performative pedagogy, we approach the practice session and the practice space within the realm of performance. We attend to specific communicative and performative moments in pedagogical contexts so we can better understand how identities are performed (and therefore produced) in ways that perpetuate, disrupt, and change social ideology and structures of power, privilege, and access. In our work as teachers and directors we draw on performance as a way to practice Freire's (1970/2000) idea of conscientization, or conscientious raising, and as a powerful mode to enact social justice.

As both a "heuristic" and an "event" performance exemplifies how culture(s) is/are produced and maintained, and offers a productive mode to enact change through generative, constitutive embodiment (Hamera 2006, p. 6). For us, performance is a "process-focused activity" in which we experiment, critique, fail, and try again (Harris 2014). Building on Pineau's (1994) conception of educational poetics, we want to extend our understandings of the ways that performances constitute educational spaces. In this book, we argue for cultivating pedagogical "practice sessions" and "practice spaces," as spaces where we help facilitate performance that works toward liberatory ends. In the following section, we offer our conceptualizations of the practice session and the practice space.

DEFINING PRACTICE SESSIONS AND SPACES

The metaphors we use to describe and define our pedagogy constitute our educational interactions (Freire 1970/2000; Lakoff and Johnson 2003; McRae 2015b; Stewart 1995; Fassett and Warren 2006). For example, when education is conceptualized as a transaction of information, or what Freire refers to as the banking model of education, teachers become responsible for delivering and depositing information to students (p. 72). The transactional metaphor constitutes educational interactions in terms of exchange and discrete units of knowledge that can be transmitted from teachers to students. This metaphor is consequential in shaping specific educational practices and values. Teachers are responsible and held accountable, for delivering information in ways that can be reproduced by students. There is a distinct separation between the teacher and the student, and curriculum, assessment, and classroom spaces are all designed in ways that reflect and reproduce this separation.

As a response to the banking model of education, Freire (1970/2000) proposes a metaphor that emphasizes interaction. He explains:

> Through dialogue, the teacher-of-the-students and the students-of-the-teacher cease to exist and a new term emerges: teacher-student with students-teachers. The teacher is no longer merely the-one-who-teachers, but one who is himself taught in dialogue with the students, who in turn while being taught also teach. They become jointly responsible for a process in which all grow. (p. 80)

The dialogic metaphor constitutes educational interactions in ways that invite a pedagogy that is emergent and that invites and creates a curriculum and classroom practice that depends on an understanding of knowledge as co-constituted amongst teachers and students.

The banking model and the dialogic approach to pedagogy presented by Freire both function metaphorically to explain and shape pedagogical interactions. These metaphors are not necessarily good or bad, nor are they neutral ways of framing what matters in education. Both of these metaphors frame educational practices in ways that are value-laden and materially consequential. Often, the metaphors that permeate educational contexts are taken-for-granted; however, as Pineau (1994) explains, metaphors can offer a starting place for designing and articulating pedagogical philosophy (pp. 12–13). In this way, developing a pedagogical metaphor offers a structural framework for theorizing and generating approaches to teaching and learning. Pineau's description of the function of metaphors in terms of pedagogy is an important call and reminder of the critical importance for educators to develop their own philosophies of teaching and learning. The ways we, as educators, theorize and explain our teaching matters politically and practically.

Our goal in this book is to advocate for the creation of a pedagogy that privileges performance and creative practices as a way of critically working toward social justice. In particular, we propose the metaphors of the practice session and the practice space as a framework for a pedagogy that features emergent and generative creative practices. If education is *like* a practice session, then ideas are generated over sustained periods of time, through repetition, and by revision and refinement. If education is *like* a practice space, then the physical and theoretical location of teaching and learning enables rehearsal and experimentation. Both the metaphor of the practice session and the practice space invite a wide range of creative approaches in educational contexts. In the following sections, we imagine the pedagogical possibilities of the practice session and practice space metaphors as they are directly related to a creative and critical approach to teaching and learning.

Practice Session

The time for practice is sacred. The practice session occurs as a ritual. It is a time set apart from the everyday. It is a time for the ceremony. It is a time that creates and follows conventions and forms. It is a time that enables change and transformation.

The time for practice is privileged time. The practice session is extraordinary. It is time for rehearsal and repetition. It is a time for experimentation and error. It is a time for revision and refinement. It is a time for making mistakes and revelations. It is a time for creating habits and possibilities. It is a time for generating styles and capacities.

The time for practice is organized and structured. The practice session is purposeful and deliberate. It is the time that is organized by routine. It is the time that is structured by the technical and systematic. It is a time that is organized by the generative and the imaginative. It is a time that is structured by the playful and spontaneous.

The time for practice is persistent. The practice session has duration. It is a time that begins and ends. The practice session has endurance. It is a time that occurs and reoccurs. The practice session has continuity. It is a time that is individual and cumulative.

The time for practice is emergent. The practice session is a process. It is a time that features the incomplete and partial. It is a time that allows for evolution and becoming. It is a time that is marked by adjustment and modification.

The time for practice is educational. The practice session is a learning opportunity. It is a time for reflection and contemplation. It is a time for understanding and comprehension. It is a time for exploration and discovery. It is a time for collaboration and connection. It is a time for examination and insight.

The practice session is a metaphor, and starting place, for theorizing a pedagogy that features and is characterized by the qualities of rehearsal in and across a variety of genres. For example, the practice session metaphor can be linked to rehearsal in the context of theater, music, sport, and ritual. First, this metaphor offers a structure for educational interactions; second, it provides a framework for the relationship amongst teachers and students; and finally, this metaphor privileges an embodied way of learning and knowing.

This metaphor first asks us to think about pedagogical interactions in terms of experimentation, repetition, and preparation. Ideas and concepts are engaged through play, understandings are developed through repetition, and positions are refined and prepared for application in a variety of different contexts. Curriculum and content are framed as dynamic materials that can be engaged from multiple perspectives. And as a practice session, teaching and learning occur as a process of creating and developing understandings that are always contingent on the experience and position of the teachers and students.

Second, this metaphor presents a relationship between teachers and students that positions the teacher as a director, a collaborator, or a mentor. The practice session presents educational interactions that may be guided and shaped by teachers. Teachers may pose questions, present routines and exercises, and offer direct suggestions and instructions. Educational interactions can also emerge as collaborations amongst teachers and students. Ideas and strategies for understanding and engaging course content may emerge in and through conversations and experimentation amongst teachers and students. With the practice session metaphor, the authority of teachers is neither absolute nor is it entirely absent.

Finally, the practice session metaphor privileges an embodied approach to teaching and learning. Ideas are presented in ways that ask students and teachers to develop their own individual connections to the content. Practice sessions frame learning as a process for generating knowledge at a bodily level. Ideas are generated collectively in and through workshops and repetitions. Practice sessions ask and expect educational interactions to involve the input, expertise, and experience of teachers *and* students. Curriculum is modified by the individual and communal experiences that emerge in the educational interaction. The metaphor of the practice session also invokes and is entangled with the metaphor of the practice space.

Practice Space

The space for practice is sacred. The practice space is a location for the ritual. It is a space set apart from the everyday. It is a space for the ceremony. It is a space for creating and following conventions and forms. It is a space that enables change and transformation.

The space for practice is privileged space. The practice space is extraordinary. It is space for rehearsal and repetition. It is a space for experimentation and error. It is a space for revision and refinement. It is a space for making mistakes and revelations. It is a space for creating habits and possibilities. It is a space for generating styles and capacities.

The space for practice is organized and structured. The practice space is designed purposefully and deliberately. It is space that can be organized by routine. It is space that is structured by the technical and systematic. It is a space that is organized by the generative and the imaginative. It is a space that is structured by the playful and spontaneous.

The space for practice is a physical location. The practice space has physical boundaries. It is a space that can be used for particular activities and movements. It is a space designed for preparation and rehearsal. It is a space that can be manipulated and modified. It is a space that can be transformed by the performances of individuals and groups.

The space for practice is educational. The practice space is a learning space. It is a space that encourages reflection and contemplation. It is a space designed for understanding and comprehension. It is a space that engenders exploration and discovery. It is a space that invites collaboration and connection. It is a space that allows for examination and insight.

The practice space is a metaphor, and starting place, for theorizing pedagogical practices and educational interactions in the context of physical locations designed for rehearsal. This metaphor imagines the physical location of educational practices, such as classrooms, as spaces for engaging in the embodied process of rehearsal. Three important implications emerge in marking the classroom and educational space as a kind of practice space. First, the practice space metaphor draws attention to the importance and impact of the physical design of educational spaces. Second, the practice space metaphor, like the practice session metaphor, provides a framework for understanding the physical relationship between teachers and students. Finally, the practice space metaphor also emphasizes and values the embodied performances that constitute educational interactions. Ultimately, the practice space is a complementary metaphor to the practice session metaphor that works toward transforming educational interactions.

The practice space metaphor first draws attention to the limits and possibilities of the physical configuration of educational spaces. If the classroom, or other educational contexts, are to be conceptualized as practice spaces, then limits and possibilities of the physical design must be considered. No single design is preferred or required to accomplish a practice space. As de Certeau (1984) contends, "space is practiced place" (p. 117). The performances of the actors (including students and teachers) in a given place create and constitute a space. However, the metaphor of the practice space raises awareness of what Kilgard (2011) refers to as the "performative possibilities" of a classroom or educational space (p. 221). It is important to understand the limits and possibilities of a physical space in terms of the kinds of practice that might be accessible and available. For instance, working in a theater space with moveable seating and lighting provides different opportunities than working in a classroom with stadium seating and fixed lighting. However, as practice spaces, each of these physical locations offers the potential to develop and enact creative possibilities. Practice spaces enable both experimentation with and presentation of ideas. Practice spaces allow for both solitary and collective acts of repetition and rehearsal. Practice spaces are dynamic, malleable, and can accommodate a variety of learning and teaching styles.

Second, the practice space metaphor informs the way the relationship between teachers and students is and can be constituted. For example, if the classroom is a practice space, then teachers and students might enter the space together as collaborators. The practice space invites a process of working, experimenting, and rehearsal that does not rely solely on the authority of teachers over students to deliver information. Teachers may work *with* students to produce and generate knowledge, understanding, and creative possibilities. It is also important to note that the practice space metaphor does not entirely erase, or ignore, the authority of the teacher in the classroom. In a practice space, teachers may also function as directors that lead and indicate directions for engagement and practice.

Finally, the metaphor of the practice space has implications for educational practices in terms of the value and emphasis that is placed on embodied performances. Practice spaces are locations where bodies can come to understand, engage, and transform concepts and ideas. Practice spaces are locations where students and teachers might come to realize the individual and communal implications of the educational curriculum. Practice spaces are also locations where play and experimentation with concepts and ideas might lead to new understandings and possibilities. By presenting and encouraging a philosophy of teaching that is grounded in the metaphors of practice sessions and spaces, we hope to invite the development of philosophies of teaching and learning that work to engage the embodied, the creative, and the critical, as a way of working toward social justice in educational practices.

ENGAGEMENT: THE CLASSROOM AS A PRACTICE SPACE
Engagement Description

The goal of this engagement to attend to the ways your pedagogical context functions as a practice space In your classroom, or pedagogical context (perhaps it is a workshop setting or reading group), with students, adjust the physical location. Set up your preferred classroom arrangement. Position furniture, chairs, lighting, sound, visuals, and personal effects, etc. Ask everyone to walk around the space. Ask students what they notice. What movement is possible? How is movement constrained? Encourage students to interact with one another in the space, perhaps directing them to a specific question, concept, or topic. Ask each person to note, or pay attention to their relationships with one another and with the space. How does talk emerge? Is there a low hum of voices? Does the building rumble? Is there virtual silence? What does physical closeness say about the space and about the relationships amongst the people present?

After taking attending to the common arrangement of the space, rearrange it. Is it possible to reposition furniture, chairs, lighting, sound, visuals, and or personal effects? Can a window be opened or the lights dimmed? Can chairs, desks, or tables move into different configurations? Can music or sound art be introduced into the space via a smart board, radio, iPhone, or having a group sing together? After rearranging the space follow the same pattern as before: Ask everyone to walk around the space. Ask students what they notice. What movement is possible? How is movement constrained? Encourage students to interact with one another in the space perhaps directing them to a specific question, concept, or topic. Ask each person to note, or pay attention to their relationships with one another and with the space. How does talk emerge? Is there a low hum of voices? Does the building rumble? Is there virtual silence? What does physical closeness say about the space and about the relationships amongst the people present?

Debriefing Questions

To debrief this engagement and connect your space to the idea of the practice space, consider the following questions:

How is Our Space Sacred?

What are the rituals we want to develop (or have developed) that frame our space? In what ways do these rituals maintain particular social norms? What are these norms? In what ways do these rituals change our space, us, or other spaces? For instance, are there routines, conventions, and forms that we follow that are similar to or different from other spaces? How do these routines, conventions, and forms affect our group in the group and beyond?

How Do We Privilege Our Space?

In what ways do we make room for rehearsal and repetition? What are the habits that we bring to the space? What habits have we created together? What is our approach to experimentation? What kinds of strategies, modes, styles, etc., are embraced here? What is our attitude toward error? Do we embrace failure(s)? When, under what circumstances?

How is Our Space Organized and Structured?

How is time or activity structured here? Who makes the rules? How are goals decided? How are plans decided? How are the structures of the space developed or imposed? Who maintains organization? When and how is structure disrupted or changed? What are the limits or boundaries? What do the limits or boundaries allow us to generate or imagine?

How Do We Understand Our Space as a Physical Location?

What does our space sound like/look like/feel like/smell like? Are there chairs and tables? Are they moveable? How much space is there for movement? Can the sound/appearance/arrangement/smell be changed? In what ways? Who has the ability (and/or power) to change the physical location? How does the physical location allow us to engage (or limit how we can engage)?

How is Our Space Educational?

What type of learning does our space enable? How do we learn in this space? What strategies, methods, and possibilities do we explore? How does the space invite us to work together? What does our space reflect? In what ways do we reflect in the space? What kinds of knowledge are encouraged here? What can we discover in, about, and from this space? What insights are produced in and by this space?

CLOSING

Educational contexts, like the classroom, can be imagined in terms of the metaphor of the practice space. What this metaphor offers is a way of framing the physical and theoretical location of teaching and learning as a space designed for a particular pedagogical approach. This is an approach to education that features and emphasizes rehearsal, repetition, and presentation. Physically, the practice space metaphor asks us to develop pedagogical approaches that attend to and notice the implications of the locations where teaching and learning happen. This metaphor also presents the opportunity for reconfiguring the spaces where we teach and learn, even if only through the most minor of adjustments.

Theoretically, the practice space is a heuristic that serves as the starting place for the overarching goals of this book. This book is a practice space for theorizing teaching and learning in terms of performance, critical pedagogy, CCP, and social justice. Theoretically, the practice space imagines teaching and learning in terms of embodiment, creative experimentation, and critical attention to social inequity. Ultimately, the practice space is a location that invites a pedagogy of practice sessions or rehearsals that work to engage in teaching, learning, and theorizing pedagogy in research. Drawing from critical performative pedagogy, we develop practice spaces and practice sessions to recognize inequity and enact social justice. In the following chapters, we invite you to engage with several different kinds of practice sessions as examples and possibilities for this creative and generative approach to teaching and learning.

REFERENCES

Alexander, B. K. (2011). Standing in the wake: A critical auto/ethnographic exercise on reflexivity in three movements. *Cultural Studies ↔ Critical Methodologies, 11*(2), 98–107. doi:10.1177/1532708611401328.

Boal, A. (1979). *Theatre of the oppressed* (C. A. McBride & M. L. McBride, Trans.). New York: Theatre Communications Group (Original work published 1974).

Butler, J. (1988). Performative acts and gender constitution: An essay in phenomenology and feminist theory. *Theatre Journal, 40,* 519–531.

Conquergood, D. (1983). Communication as performance: Dramaturgical dimensions of everyday life. In J. Sisco (Ed.), *The Jensen lectures: Contemporary communication studies* (pp. 24–43). Tampa: University of South Florida.

Conquergood, D. (2002). Performance studies: Interventions and radical research. *TDR: The Drama Review, 46*(2), 145–156.

Cooks, L. (2010). The (critical) pedagogy of communication and the (critical) communication of pedagogy. In D. L. Fassett & J. T. Warren (Eds.), *The SAGE handbook of communication and instruction* (pp. 293–314). Thousand Oaks, CA: Sage.

de Certeau, M. (1984). *The practice of everyday life* (S. Rendall, Trans.). Berkeley: University of California Press.

Dolan, J. (1996). Producing knowledges that matter: Practicing performance studies through theatre studies. *The Drama Review, 40,* 9–19.

Eisner, E. W. (2004). What can education learn from the arts about the practice of education? *International Journal of Education & the Arts, 5*, 1–12.

Fassett, D. L., & Warren, J. T. (2006). *Critical communication pedagogy*. Thousand Oaks, CA: Sage.

Féral, J. (2012). How to define presence effects: The work of Janet Cardiff. In G. Giannachi, N. Kaye, & M. Shanks (Eds.), *Archaeologies of presence: Art, performance, and the persistence of being* (pp. 29–49). New York: Routledge.

Freire, P. (2000). *Pedagogy of the oppressed* (30th anniversary ed.) (M. B. Ramos, Trans.). New York: Continuum (Original work published 1970).

Geertz, C. (1973). Thick description: Toward an interpretive theory of culture. In C. Geertz (Ed.), *The interpretation of culture* (pp. 3–30). New York: Basic Books.

Grande, S. (2004). *Red pedagogy: Native American social and political thought*. Lantham, MD: Rowman and Littlefield.

Hamera, J. (2006). Introduction: Opening *opening acts*. In J. Hamera (Ed.), *Opening acts: Performance in/as communication* (pp. 1–10). Thousand Oaks, CA: Sage.

Harris, A. (2014). *The creative turn: Toward a new aesthetic imaginary*. Rotterdam: Sense Publishers.

Henshaw, V. (2013). *Urban smellscapes: Understanding and designing city smell environments*. Hoboken: Taylor and Francis.

Hytten, K. (2006). Education for social justice: Provocations and challenges. *Educational Theory, 56*(2), 221–236.

Kilgard, A. K. (2011). Chaos as praxis: Or, troubling performance pedagogy: Or, you are now. *Text and Performance Quarterly, 31*, 217–228.

Kincheloe, J. (2008). *Critical pedagogy primer* (2nd ed.). New York: Peter Lang.

Lakoff, G., & Johnson, M. (2003). *Metaphors we live by* (2nd ed.). Chicago: University of Chicago Press.

Leder, D. (1990). *The absent body*. Chicago: The University of Chicago Press.

McLaren, P. (1999). *Schooling as ritual performance: Toward a political economy of educational symbols and gestures* (3rd ed.). New York: Rowman & Littlefield (Original work published 1986).

McRae, C. (2015a). Hearing performance as music. *Liminalities: A Journal of Performance Studies, 11*(5), 1–19.

McRae, C. (2015b). *Performative listening: Hearing others in qualitative research*. New York: Peter Lang.

Pascoe, C. J. (2007). *Dude you're a fag: Masculinity and sexuality in high school*. Berkeley: University of California Press.

Pelias, R. J. (2014). *Performance: An alphabet of performative writing*. Walnut Creek, CA: Left Coast Press.

Pelias, R. J., & Van Oosting, J. (1987). A paradigm for performance studies. *Quarterly Journal of Speech, 73*, 219–231.

Pineau, E. L. (1994). Teaching is performance: Reconceptualizing a problematic metaphor. *American Educational Research Journal, 31*(1), 3–25.

Pineau, E. L. (1995). Re-casting rehearsal: Making a case for production as research. *Journal of the Illinois Speech and Theatre Association, 46*, 43–52.

Pineau, E. L. (2002). Critical performative pedagogy: Fleshing out the politics of liberatory education. In N. Stucky & C. Wimmer (Eds.), *Teaching performance studies* (pp. 41–54). Carbondale: Southern Illinois University Press.

Sensoy, O., & DiAngelo, R. (2012). *Is everyone really equal?: An introduction to key concepts in social justice education.* New York: Teachers College Press.

Stewart, J. (1995). *Language as articulate contact: Towards a post semiotic philosophy of communication.* Albany, NY: SUNY Press.

Stewart, K. (2011). Atmospheric attunements. *Environment and Planning D: Society and Space, 29*, 445–453.

Stucky, N., & Wimmer, C. (2002). Introduction: The power of transformation in performance studies pedagogy. In N. Stucky & C. Wimmer (Eds.), *Teaching performance studies* (pp. 1–32). Carbondale: Southern Illinois University Press.

Taylor, D. (2003). *The archive and the repertoire: Performing cultural memory in the Americas.* Durham: Duke University Press.

Warren, J. T. (1999). The body politic: Performance, pedagogy, and the power of enfleshment. *Text and Performance Quarterly, 19*, 257–266.

Warren, J. T. (2003). *Performing purity: Whiteness, pedagogy, and the reconstitution of power.* New York: Peter Lang.

Warren, J. T., & Fassett, D. L. (2010). Critical communication pedagogy: Reframing the field. In D. L. Fassett & J. T. Warren (Eds.), *The Sage handbook of communication and instruction* (pp. 283–292). Thousand Oaks, CA: Sage.

Westerkamp, H. (1974). Soundwalking. *Sound Heritage, 3*, 18–27.

Willis, P. (1981). *Learning to labor: How working class kids get working class jobs.* New York: Columbia University Press.

CHAPTER 3

Performance as Research

In this chapter, we describe the first of our five practice sessions. This first practice session focuses on the practice of the performance workshop. We specifically feature performance and performance workshops as a way of conducting and staging research questions. We contend that performance workshops provide the space for generating new insights about and possibilities for human interaction and communication. We begin by articulating three characteristics of performance workshops. First, performance workshops emphasize embodiment and experimentation. Second, performance workshops offer space to generate new perspectives. Third, performance workshops prioritize interaction amongst participants and therefore function as exercises in making community.

After describing the characteristics of performance workshops, we then discuss how performance workshops can function as acts of research, connection across difference, and as transformation. We specifically forward the argument for performance as way to administer research and to stage research questions. We also focus on the ways performance provides the space for creating and sharing understandings across difference. Finally, as an act of critical pedagogy, the performance workshop also functions to develop an awareness of the status quo and provides the opportunity to imagine possibilities for change. Throughout this chapter, we theorize the ways performance workshops function as a creative practice for teaching and learning in the service of social justice. We also provide several possible workshop prompts and ideas for engaging in performance as a way of extending and expanding various research questions.

© The Author(s) 2017
C. McRae and A. Huber, *Creating Performances for Teaching and Learning*,
Creativity, Education and the Arts, DOI 10.1007/978-3-319-54561-5_3

Agenda

1. Warm-up
2. Three characteristics of performance workshops
3. Performance workshop as research
4. Performance workshop as contact/connection
5. Performance workshop as transformation
6. Engagement: Creating a performance workshop
7. Closing

WARM-UP

Tuning into Pedagogical Spaces

This first practice session begins, like all of our practices, with an invitation to warm-up. In this warm-up, we turn our attention to the pedagogical possibilities of our various spaces. For instance, how can our space function as a location for learning? For teaching? For education? What do you need from a space in order to begin learning? To begin teaching? Using the following questions as a guide, we urge you to create a running list of how you cultivate teaching and learning spaces.

Take a deep breath.

Exhale.

Wiggle your fingers. Wiggle your toes.

What characterizes a learning space?

How might you name different learning spaces? Are you in a theater? A classroom? A laboratory? A conference room? An office? A studio? A study? A bedroom? A kitchen? A garage? A library? A lobby? A coffee shop? A restaurant? A bar? An open-air arena? A field? A park?

What exists in your learning space?

Desks? Chairs? A stage? A podium? A projector? A television? A sound system? A smart board? A chalkboard? A whiteboard? A computer? Books? Easels? Platforms? Reader's Theater blocks? A table? A workbench? Cushions? Athletic Equipment?

How is your learning space organized? Is there open space? Are supplies and furniture arranged in particular ways? Are desks and tables in a circle, or in rows, or grouped together, or some other configuration? Does the space encourage collaboration or independent work or both?

Take a deep breath.

Exhale.

Wiggle your fingers. Wiggle your toes.

What do you bring to your learning space?

What's in your bag? What's at your desk? What surrounds your favorite study corner, cubby, or chair? Do you have a pencil? A pen? A pencil sharpener? Extra ink refills? A stapler? Paper clips? A device (smart phone, tablet, computer)? A giant eraser? A ruler? A highlighter? A composition notebook? A spiral-bound notebook? Post-it notes? Post-it flags? Bookmarks? Headphones?

Do you bring a snack? Something to drink? A sweater or a jacket? Do you bring a child? A pet? A friend? A partner? Do you bring your worries? Your joys? Your curiosity? Your patience? Your self-restraint? Your nervousness?

Take a deep breath.

Exhale.

Wiggle your fingers. Wiggle your toes.

What characterizes a space for teaching?

What's in your bag? Books? Notes? An outline? A set of markers? A padfolio? A binder of exercises? A computer? An electronic file of course materials on a cloud or institutional server? A flash drive? A computer-generated slideshow? A clipboard? Examples ? A video clip? A song? Comfortable shoes? Glasses? Contacts? Hearing aids?

Do you bring a snack or something to drink? A sweater? A coat? An umbrella? Do you bring sunglasses? Do you bring guest teachers or co-teachers? Do you bring too much? Are you loaded down with canvas bags? Do you bring too little? Do you forget things at your desk or at your house? Do you bring anxiety? Anticipation? Worry? Do you bring passion? Curiosity? Answers? Questions?

Take a deep breath.

Exhale.

Wiggle your fingers. Wiggle your toes.

How do you create productive learning spaces?

Where do you struggle to learn? What kinds of spaces make learning challenging for you? Do you struggle to concentrate in spaces that are too small? Too big? Spaces that are crowded? Spaces with many bodies? Spaces that confine movement? Spaces that require movement? How is your focus affected by smells, sounds, sights, and textures?

What is your ideal space for teaching and learning? What spaces are most generative for you? Where do you learn best? Do you learn in a quiet space? Do you learn in a space filled with noise? Filled with other bodies? Do you learn best by yourself? In small groups? In large workshops?

Do you learn best in desks? Or, while moving? Or, while reading? Or, while taking notes? Or, while listening? Or, while discussing? Or, while painting? Or, while writing? Is your best learning style some combination of the above, or something different all together?

Take a deep breath.

Exhale.

Wiggle your fingers. Wiggle your toes.

Debriefing the Warm-up

All places present the possibility to function as pedagogical spaces. Performances of learning and teaching may occur anywhere from restaurants, to classrooms, to libraries, to parks, or private offices. The prompts in this warm-up are aimed at generating an awareness of the expectations and taken-for-granted assumptions that you might have about learning spaces and about what constitutes a productive space for learning. Some of our prompts may resonate directly with your assumptions about learning spaces. However, because spaces of learning always emerge contextually and culturally, it is more likely that these prompts offer a starting place for you to generate your own catalogs of the meaningful characteristics of learning spaces. This warm-up also functions as a starting place for establishing a link between practice spaces and practice sessions. The practice space is a specific kind of learning space that is constituted by and works to enable performances of rehearsal, investigation, and experimentation.

WARMING-UP AS GENERATIVE PROCESS

Alexander (2000) introduces the concept of the generative autobiography as a process for engaging and responding to autobiographical performances by developing new performances. The characteristics of this theory help articulate the generative function and focus of our warm-up activity. For Alexander, generative autobiographical performance is a way of explaining and theorizing the creation of a performance response to autobiographical performances. He explains:

> Generative autobiography empowers and sanctions those who audience the performance of autobiography and personal narrative, especially

performance studies scholars and students of performance. The charge is to use their articulated knowledge of human communication, performance theory and method, combined with their specified/engaged positionality in the audience, to engage the performance critically. The performance becomes an opportunity not only to empathize with the performer, the constructed autobiographical self in the performance, or to critique the effectiveness of the aesthetic act, but to use the occasion of autobiographical performance, with its varying nuances, as an opportunity for personal reflection and cultural critique. (p. 110)

Generative autobiographical performances are performances that emerge from the experience of witnessing the provocative performance of others. In other words, autobiographical performances enable the creation of new autobiographical performances as responses, critiques, and extensions.

The prompting and guiding questions featured in our warm-up activity are designed and offered with the hope of engendering what might be called a generative performance response. The questions we pose function to represent a *possible* starting place for generating your own catalog of the characteristics of learning spaces. In terms of Alexander's (2000) conception of generative autobiography, these warm-up questions are designed with the hope of both triggering memory *and* generating autobiographical reflection (p. 101). In other words, our prompts may lead you to think about specific qualities of learning spaces that you encounter or have encountered in the past. These prompts are also offered as a starting place for you to begin reflecting on your own experiences of learning.

In addition to prompting generative responses, our warm-up is also a particularly cultural act. The questions we pose are necessarily cultural and indicative of *our* lived experiences within spaces of learning (Alexander 1998, pp. 178–179). In other words, the questions we offer are not the only way to go about identifying the characteristics and qualities of learning spaces. The warm-up activity, like all educational activity, is always marked by a cultural position. In this instance, our warm-up is particularly marked by our cultural identities as performance scholars who both teach and work in a public university. The kinds of learning spaces we tend to notice are often connected to and located within educational institutions. Similarly, the way we go about noticing learning spaces is marked by our disciplinary commitments to performance studies and critical pedagogy. What we notice about learning spaces tends to deal with questions of embodiment and micro-practices, as well as with larger enabling and constraining structural features.

The format of our warm-up activity (the questions and prompts) is aimed at generating responses and personal reflections. The specific content of this warm-up is designed to draw attention to the ways learning spaces might emerge and function for you. Particularly, we are interested in considering the function and form of spaces for learning through practice. What spaces enable your own practices of learning? What are the characteristics of these spaces? How do different spaces allow different approaches to learning? What spaces challenge your thinking? What spaces offer a sense of comfort? What spaces do you find yourself drawn to as a student? By attending to and accounting for the spaces that engender learning we can begin to cultivate these spaces for specific practices and rituals of learning. In the following section, we discuss how space may be cultivated to into particular practice sessions, such as the performance workshop.

THREE CHARACTERISTICS OF PERFORMANCE WORKSHOPS

Our first practice session is the performance workshop. Performance workshops are spaces for embodied and staged pedagogical interactions. Performance workshops offer a space for experimenting with and exploring ideas, ideology, and cultural phenomena. In other words, performance workshops encourage conceptual play. Performance workshops also offer a space for developing, devising, and refining conceptual understandings into tangible products or productions. In other words, performance workshops encourage creative and generative acts.

Our understanding of the performance workshop emerges from the traditions of theater, performance studies, and performance art (Boal, 1979, 1992; Bogart and Lanau 2005; Bogart 2007; Bottoms and Goulish 2007; Bowman and Bowman 2002; Pineau 1995; Pelias 1999; Pelias and Shaffer 2007; Spry 2011; Yordon 1997). However, performance experience is not needed in order to enact or engage with the performance workshop as a pedagogical strategy. In what follows we discuss three distinct characteristics that inform our definition of the performance workshop. First, the performance workshop is characterized as embodied and experimental. Second, the performance workshop is characterized by an emphasis on cultivating new perspectives. Third, the performance workshop highlights interaction and community building.

Characteristic 1: Embodied Process/Experimentation

The first characteristic of performance workshops is an emphasis on embodiment and experimentation. Performance workshops draw attention to the ways in which lived experience is always embodied. These workshops also accentuate the ways that bodies function and come to be in relationship to one another and larger cultural contexts. Performance workshops require embodied experimentation and play. Unlike other workshops, performance workshops are dependent upon participants' willingness to engage corporeally. As opposed to workshops that ask participants to generate written work, or extend ideas, performance workshops not only encourage participants to play, craft, and develop ideas, these workshops emphasize the ways bodies contribute to, create, and engage with the world. To engage corporeally means to privilege the work of the body, be it through embodied movement, knowledge, and/or experience.

This emphasis on embodiment within performance workshops re-centers the body and therefore asks participants to engage and experiment with affect. Centering on the body allows participants to engage with their senses. Participants are encouraged to make meaningful connections between the complexities of what their bodies feel and know. Embodied experimentation also asks participants to take risks, be flexible and straddle tenuous boundaries between comfort and apprehension. Pushing beyond what is comfortable offers new insights not only about the self or the individual, but also about the context(s) and communities in which participants live.

Within a performance workshop, embodied experimentation happens in different ways and forms. Workshop leaders may decide to focus on a particular theme, which will then affect the methods they choose to facilitate embodiment. Workshop leaders may also decide they want to work within particular constraints to test the limits of what bodies are capable of doing. With both novice and experienced performers, we strive to develop a routine of embodied practice to enable corporeal play. We want performers to become comfortable in their bodies and begin developing a habit for engaging in bodily experimentation. Embodied experimentation takes many forms and often includes developing vocal expression, movement, and interaction with other bodies. For example, in the workshops we facilitate, we cultivate vocal expression by working with producing sound, playing with articulation and pronunciation, and providing opportunities for participants to simply practice words and written selections out loud.

Characteristic 2: New Perspectives

The second characteristic of the performance workshop is the emphasis on generating new perspectives. Performance workshops are opportunities for experimentation, play, and rehearsal in the service of discovering and encountering new insights and perspectives about the topics, questions, or projects that participants engage. Although performance workshops may vary from topic to topic, the process is designed to enable participants to encounter new ways of approaching, appreciating, or questioning the content at hand. In other words, performance workshops are distinctly pedagogical. They are learning opportunities.

The recognition of performance workshops as pedagogical is important because this establishes an ethic for the kinds of work and focus of the workshop practice. Participants in performance workshops are asked to take an open stance and position as students and learners. Performance workshops are designed to encourage discovery and learning that is not predetermined. Ideas and revelations might be discovered in various moments throughout the workshop, and/or new insights might be realized in moments of reflection and debriefing immediately following specific activities.

In order to encourage the development of new perspectives, performance workshops are designed to invite participants to engage in acts of research, revision, and reflection. Throughout the performance workshops, opportunities are offered for participants to experiment with and modify their ideas. For example, in our performance workshops we often ask participants to make adjustments to their projects based on feedback they receive from the workshop leaders or from the other participants. We also often provide opportunities for participants to reflect on and debrief the activities and events of the workshop. This might include prompts for individual writing responses or open-ended questions for group discussion. The learning that might occur during a performance workshop will vary from participant to participant, and topic to topic, but ultimately the workshops are always presented as practices for learning.

Characteristic 3: Interaction and Community Building

The final characteristic of the performance workshop is an emphasis on interaction and community building. Performance workshops are designed to create opportunities for engaging with the ideas of others in two distinct ways. First, performance workshops are spaces for interacting with the ideas of others that may not necessarily be physically present in the workshop. For example, a performance workshop is a space for considering the implications of various texts, theories, and perspectives of others in ways that are embodied and experimental. The second way that performance workshops offer the opportunity for interaction with the ideas of others is by inviting participants to collaborate, critique, and create with each other. Performance workshops are spaces where ideas are not only developed, but they are witnessed and responded to by the participants.

This emphasis on interaction with the ideas of others also allows for the development of new and even unexpected insights. Sustained engagement with the texts, theories, and perspectives of others may lead to the development of new ways of thinking and understanding. Interacting with other workshop participants also creates the opportunity for a sense of community to emerge amongst participants. In the context of the performance workshop, ideas and practices are not solitary accomplishments; rather, they are always shaped and informed by the dynamic of the workshop participants. The collaborative nature of the performance workshop highlights a kind of creative process that values the process of giving and receiving feedback as a central component to the development of creative projects.

In order to emphasize this kind of interaction amongst participants, performance workshops are typically designed in such a way that includes time for interaction amongst participants in pairs or small groups. This time might be organized to include collaborative generation of ideas (or brainstorming), sharing and presenting of work, and descriptive feedback and critique. A discussion about the expectations for the kinds of feedback and critique might further help to structure these interactions. For example, in our performance workshops we typically ask participants to always begin their feedback in terms that are descriptive and non-evaluative. This approach allows the performers to begin hearing how their work is being witnessed so that they can begin to make changes that address specific concerns and observations (rather than trying to address critiques that are often more abstract and vague).

Performance workshops are characterized by the emphasis on embodiment, the development of new perspectives, and interaction with the ideas of others. In the following sections, we discuss how we define and develop performance workshops as acts of research, connection across difference, and transformation.

PERFORMANCE WORKSHOP AS RESEARCH

Performance, as an artistic practice, provides the space for generating new insights about and possibilities for human interaction and communication. Contemporary performance research provides a framework for how we can begin to understand the performance workshop as research. For instance, performance can be an experimental form of conducting research (Bowman and Bowman 2002). Similarly, performance can offer creative way of staging research questions (Madison 1999). The process of crafting and developing performance can also be a process of discovery (Pineau 1995). Performance is a rich method of inquiry and mode of engaging in research. *Performance workshops* are spaces for practicing and engaging in performance as a form of researching the world and human interaction (Huber and McRae 2014). In this discussion, we are particularly interested in demonstrating the ways performance workshops can be designed to engage in the process of research through exploration, explanation, and exaggeration.

Exploration

The first step in designing a performance workshop for research is to engage in a practice of exploration. This step will enable participants to begin describing, defining, and exploring the world. This first step depends on and demands careful observation. To begin to explore the world, participants must pay careful attention to their surroundings. For instance, participants may consider what is happening in and around their homes, in their relationship, and in their communities. The specific topic or focus of the observations may change depending on the focus of the workshop or the individual participants. In the workshop, observations are guided by various prompts, activities, and questions.

Consider the following instructions for a performance workshop designed to explore the world. First, invite participants to make observations using various forms or methods of documentation that might include the following: writing, drawing, photography, painting, sculpture, collage, video-recording, sound recording, interviews, etc. Second, provide participants with specific instructions and guidelines for conducting their observations. The goal of this process is to provide participants with an opportunity to explore particular phenomenon (such as human interactions, cultural practices, discourses) in a way that can lead to insights into what exists in the world, i.e., "what is." Like other research practices, which document and gather data for further interpretation, observation within the performance workshop provides the participant with evidence for interpretation and analysis.

For example, instruct participants to:

• Use writing utensils or digital devices to create a written account of their surroundings.
• Use markers, crayons, pens, and pencils to draw the phenomenon they are observing.
• Use molding clay to sculpt the phenomenon they are observing.
• Use pictures to create a collage as a form of documentation.
• Use audio-recording devices to record their observations.
• Use video-recording devices to aid in the observation process.
• Use written language to list, narrate, describe, and poeticize the phenomenon they are witnessing.

Additional instructions for observation can be offered including time limits or reminders for participants to attend to specific sensory qualities in their documentation (for example, smells, sounds, textures, tastes, and sights).

Explanation

The second step in designing a workshop for research is to engage in explanation. This step will enable participants to begin to explain and interpret their observations. To begin to explain the world and interpret what they have documented, workshop participants must attend to the ways that they interpret initial observations. They should consider how their own lived experience influences their observations. For instance, participants may consider how their observations are situated in particular social, political, and cultural contexts. Participants may consider their own particular experiences that are similar to or different from what they observe. They may also consider how specific cultural values influence their understanding of particular situations. Facilitators may also help focus interpretations through prompts, questions, and activities.

In guiding this step of the workshop, consider the subsequent instructions. First, ask participants to offer descriptions about their documented observations. Then, prompt them to develop interpretations or analysis about their observations. This can include the creation of comparisons, analogies, or metaphors that might extend or broaden their initial observations. The goal of this process is to begin to "explain the world" by developing workshop participants' meaning-making process. Additionally, guide participants to consider the ways their own interpretive frameworks, cultural positions, and individual perspectives shape their analysis and explanations (Pelias and Shaffer 2007, pp. 181–195).

For example, ask participants to:

- Describe documented observations in concrete terms that attend to relationships amongst terms and figures.
- Describe documented observations in ways that attend to shapes, colors, sounds, and textures.
- Describe and catalog words or themes that are intriguing and/or curious.
- Describe documented observations created by other workshop participants.

Based on these descriptions prompt participants to develop interpretations and analysis of their initial observations through specific questions such as:

- What phenomenon are these observations related to?
- What are contrasting phenomena?
- What metaphors or language might be used to explain these descriptions?

Finally, guide participants to reflexively consider the ways their interpretive frameworks, cultural positions, and individual perceptions inform their explanations. Encourage participants to "notice how they notice." All observations are made through the particular lens of the observer. Nothing is neutral. The goal here is that participants to begin attending to their lens by investigating the impact of their privileges, tendencies, and experiences on their research practices.

Exaggeration

The final step in designing a performance workshop as an act of research is for participants to begin developing their observations and interpretations for presentation. The staging and performing of research is a unique aspect of performance as a research method, and the performance workshop provides an introduction to this method. It is important to note that there are multiple strategies and possibilities for staging performance research. However, for the purposes of our discussion we offer what we refer to as exaggeration or amplification, as one strategy for engaging the presentational possibilities of performance.

Converting interpretations and observations into an embodied presentation allows participants the opportunity to develop new insights about the phenomenon or topic at hand. To facilitate the turn toward performance, consider the following instructions. First, ask participants to review their observations and interpretations to locate emergent and recurring themes. Encourage participants to consider initial ideas that have stayed with them and developed throughout the workshop process. Second, prompt participants to select themes to develop into a performance piece. Ask each participant to cultivate the theme in a way that exaggerates or amplifies it. Strategies used to help participants develop this stage of the performance workshop may include, but are not limited to: employment of repetition (of words, phrases, movement, images, etc.), juxtaposition, and incorporation of media, collage, and montage. The workshop facilitator, as well as specific focus of the workshop, will help determine further boundaries or requirements of the performance.

For example, guide participants to:

- Develop an observation or interpretation into a text for presentation.
- Revise the text to incorporate the use of repetition of phrases to highlight a specific theme.
- Create corresponding gestures or movements for their presentational text.
- Develop a task or activity to be enacted while presenting their selected text.
- Develop a series of movements or gestures that highlight a theme or observation without the use of a spoken text.
- Incorporate a series of outside texts (or themes) that provide a juxtaposition for the theme being developed.
- Create a collage of images, or montage of video segments that amplifies a particular observation or theme.

Provide additional guidelines and instructions including time limits, requirements for use of space, props, and movement. Consider offering specific instructions for creating presentations in order to direct participants toward the accomplishment of particular goals.

For instance, direct participants to:

- Create a presentation that is no longer than 5 mins(or other time restriction).
- Create a presentation that uses at least one repeated gesture.
- Incorporate at least one repeated phrase or word.
- Incorporate one prop that has multiple functions.
- Generate at least three levels of composition (i.e., sitting, standing, leaning, kneeling, etc.).
- Incorporate different levels of light, and/or sound.
- Make a deliberate costuming choice.
- Include a set number of citations (from, e.g., current events, lyrics, blog, menu items, political speeches, academic articles, etc.).
- Include a set number of bodies (i.e., solo or group performance).
- Include audience participation.
- Develop this presentation in no more than 7 mins.

The use of these specific rules and instructions not only helps guide the choices the performers make, but they also offer a set of constraints that serve to focus the creative process. Workshop facilitators may also coordinate collaboration amongst participants throughout the preparation process. This may include opportunities for feedback, brainstorming, and rehearsal amongst participants.

PERFORMANCE WORKSHOP AS CONTACT

Performance workshops may be designed as a kind of research process that includes exploring, explaining, and exaggerating or amplifying various phenomena. These workshops can result in the creation of new discoveries, insights, and embodied ways of knowing the world. Performance workshops as embodied ways of knowing, developing new perspectives, and creating community can also be designed with the specific goal of providing the space for creating and sharing understandings across difference. In other words, performance workshops can serve as practices for developing contact and connection with others.

In his discussion of the moral dimensions of performance ethnography, Conquergood (1985) emphasizes the value and importance of dialogic engagement in research that centers on and engages others (p. 9). For Conquergood, dialogic engagement is a stance that "struggles to bring together different voices, world views, value systems and beliefs so that they can have a conversation with one another" (p. 9). This conversational position characterizes the ways performance, as a method of research, invites engagement across difference. In her discussion of the similarities between writing and performance, Dolan (2005) articulates the ways performance functions to engage and encounter others. She states, "Writing, like performance, lets me try on, try out, experiment with another site of anticipation, which is the moment of intersubjective relation between word and eye, between writer and reader, all based on the exchange of empathy, respect, and desire" (p. 168). Performance, and for Dolan writing, are modes that open up the space for creating and developing understandings about and recognition of others.

This stance of empathy, conversation, and connection informs our design of performance workshops as specific practices of creating contact with others. These workshops are designed to engage performance research that is specifically focused on understanding and engaging the texts, lived experiences, and communicative interactions and utterances of others. For example, this might include creating performances in which performers engage with others through esthetic texts, interviews, and/or ethnographic accounts. The performance workshop as contact specifically considers the micro-practices of others and the macrostructures that shape and inform these practices. These workshops are also designed to encourage reflexivity amongst participants in their interactions with the ideas, positions, and experiences of others.

Micro-Practices

Pelias and Shaffer's (2007) frame of empathy helps to situate our discussion of contact and is a starting place for examining the micro-practices of others. Pelias and Shaffer explain empathy as a three-step process of recognition, convergence, and adoption, in which a performer identifies everyday micro-practices in order to try to understand the other, then takes on or performs those micro-practices to feel what it might be like to be the other, and finally incorporates the other's way of seeing/understanding into their own world view (pp. 102–107). Therefore, in order to generate opportunities for connection, workshop participants need to strive for understanding of others. They begin to do this through an examination of the micro-practices of others. Micro-practices include day-to-day activities, language, conversations, and routines of others.

The types of micro-practices participants will be able to observe and examine will depend on the type of performance project in which participants are engaging. For instance, if participants are working strictly with esthetic texts (i.e., poetry, prose, letters, and essays), they may be limited to the written micro-practices that exist only in the text, or documented research about the text. Whereas, if participants are working with an ethnographic account, they may have access to the people who generate the micro-practices and therefore daily routines, rituals, conversations, as well as documented field notes and research.

Consider the following instructions to develop a performance workshop centered on contact and connections. In terms of examining the micro-practices of others, prompt participants to review the performance materials and initial research to identify common practices of the other or others. For instance, ask participants to look at repeated activities, routines, and language or phrases. Guide them to also focus on a specific or significant event or conflict. For instance, encourage participants to describe particular micro-practices that reveal something about the event or conflict and the other or others. Ask participants examine micro-practices in terms of identification and performance.

IDENTIFYING MICRO-PRACTICES

First, advise participants to identify the micro-practices of the other. Ask them to consider the other with whom they are trying to make contact. Instruct them to consider their data and artifacts. How much material do they have? Are they working within a single text (i.e., a poem)? Do they have additional research about the text? Or, are they working with ethnographic evidence, such as field notes and continued access to a particular group? The type of data and amount of material the participants have will help them determine how and where they will begin to sift through and identify micro-practices. For instance, if participants are working with only a single text, they will not have as much information to sift through, but it might also be more difficult to find patterns.

When examining materials, guide participants to consider what kinds of things jump out at them. Are there specific words or phrases used in particular ways? Prompt the participants to see whether they can decipher what these things mean? When and where is specific language used? Ask the participants to specify how they understand the language used? How is this usage different from or similar to the participants' own experience(s)?

Additionally, ask participants to mark the routines or activities they encounter in terms of the other. For example, what types of routines or activities do they notice? What types of things are involved in these routines/activities? Who performs these routines/activities? When are these routines/activities performed? How do participants understand these routines/activities? Are they similar to routines/activities the participants have experienced?

PERFORMING MICRO-PRACTICES

Not only do performance workshops offer strategies for examining micro-practices of others, the real significance of these workshops is the ways in which they facilitate contact and connection through performance. In other words, participants begin developing contact and connection with others through embodied performance. Participants can "take on" and perform others by putting these micro-practices in their own bodies. In doing so, participants are able to gain insights into the embodied actions of others.

For instance, if participants are working with an ethnographic project or esthetic artifact, workshop leaders may direct participants to embody one micro-practice, taking on a particular phrase and action, and repeating it over a specific amount time. The rehearsal of a singular micro-practice will enable the performer to experiment with elements of voice, like volume, tone, rate, and pitch, as well as elements of embodiment, such as physical levels, gesture, movement, and touch. By rehearsing these micro-practices, the workshop participants can begin to learn not only what it might be like for the other to participate in particular activities, but the ways in which these practices are connected to and influenced by their own practices.

Another strategy for performing the micro-practices of others includes asking workshop participants perform the stories of one another. For instance, direct each participant to craft a brief personal narrative, which s/he will then recount to a partner or small group. Then direct the person or persons who have audienced the narrative to re-perform what they have witnessed. The audience member(s) preparing the re-performance of the story will need to pay close attention to the story itself, but also how the story is being told, in terms of the use of words, phrases, body language, movement, gesture, and emphasis. Depending on time, participants may be able to hear narratives more than once before developing, rehearsing, and presenting the re-performance of the story.

This strategy will give workshop participants direct access to the experience and words of another. It also ensures that the other person is present for the performance, which can help performers to be accountable for their performance choices. By this, we do not mean to say there is some sort of objective authenticity that can be achieved in performance. Rather, when trying to engage with others through performance, it is important to strive for conscientious portrayals of those being performed.

Macrostructures

Individual and everyday practices always emerge and are enacted in particular contexts or structures. Hall (1985) defines this relationship between micro-practices and macrostructures as double articulation. He explains:

> By "double articulation" I mean that the structure—the given conditions of existence, the structure of determinations in any situation—can also be understood from another point of view, as simply the result of previous practices. We may say that a structure is what previously structured practices have produced as a result. (p. 95)

In other words, structures constitute practices and practices constitute structures. Developing an awareness of this relationship is significant because it asks performers to consider not only the actions of others, but also the ways these actions are always enabled and constrained by various cultural, institutional, and social conditions.

Recognizing and accounting for the relationship between structures and practices can enable a fuller appreciation for the actions, perspectives, and positions of others as always occurring in relationship to other structures. In other words, accounting for structural and systemic conditions engenders a nuanced recognition of the actions of others as always more than just emerging from a set of individual intentions. Furthermore, accounting for structures and systems also enables an acknowledgement of the ways individual practices participate in the creation of larger cultural, institutional, and social structures (Hall 1985, pp. 95–96).

Performing Macrostructures

Consider the following questions and prompts to begin accounting for the relationship between practices of others and larger structures:

First, ask participants to identify the specific context for this particular set of actions, words, or practices that they are engaging. Have them generate a list all of the possible ways they might characterize or name this context. For example, is this an institutional context (a school, a business organization, a religious institution, etc.), a relational context (a family, a friendship, a partnership, etc.), a social context (a neighborhood, a digital space, a public location), a legal context (a site of policy dispute or law enforcement, etc.), or some other cultural context (a political interaction, a ritual, a group formation, etc.)?

Next, using the physical workshop space, guide participants to map out the imagined boundaries and borders of this context or "cultural stage" (Bell 2008, p. 131). Urge them to begin by walking/moving around the space. Provide participants with the following instructions:

- Walking at a moderate pace, take the time to notice and fill the empty and available spaces around you without running into any of the other participants.
- As you walk begin to imagine and respond to the textures, boundaries, and features that characterize the particular context you are engaging. For example, does this context present physical barriers that you must navigate?
- Would this context cause you to change your pace, posture, or gestures? Does this context, or location, require the use of particular equipment, props, or costumes?

After participants finish exploring the space as an imagined cultural stage for the actions or practices they are considering, have them discuss their realizations about this context with other participants. Ask them, how this particular context, physical location, or cultural stage enables or constrains particular actions? What are the limitations of this context? What are the expectations, or norms, for interaction in this space?

Finally, prompt participants to consider the ways this context is realized through particular practices of the performers who inhabit this context. In other words, how do individual actions contribute to the limiting and enabling features of a particular context?

This engagement is one way performance workshop participants may begin to further consider the significance and implications of the choices and actions of others through embodied performance. By physically mapping and imagining the boundaries and challenges of particular contexts, participants can begin to explore and question the ways micro-practices emerge in relationship with larger structures and systems.

Reflexivity

The performance workshop as an opportunity for creating contact with others is a creative practice that engages in and emerges from an other-centered ethic that values difference. Conquergood's (1985) call for dialogic engagement provides a communicative metaphor for theorizing the ways performance enables interaction with the ideas, positions, and experiences of others. Empathetically identifying and engaging with the micro-practices of others establishes points of connection and contact with others. Using performance to consider and realize the macrostructures and systems that enable and constrain the micro-practices of others allows participants to develop a nuanced appreciation of the positions and experiences of others.

The performance workshop, a means of developing contact or connection with others, also allows participants to engage in an embodied act of reflexivity. By performing and embodying the action and, words of others, and by considering the embodied consequences of structures and contexts, performers may come to know and appreciate the experience of others. However, what is more likely, and important, is that these performance engagements will lead to the possibility for participants to recognize the ways their own positions, privileges, and experiences inform their interactions with others. In his discussion of the ethical significance of the philosophy of Emmanuel Levinas, Arnett (2008) explains:

> When we assume we know the reason for our own actions or that of another, we invite a terror between persons. When we conclude we know the truth about the Other and impose it upon that other, we invite a terror of inquiry. When totality trumps infinity, we invite a terror of categories, forgetting that, at times totality must trump to keep its secondary status. Otherwise, one turns infinity into a totality. (p. 85)

Following Arnett's caution, performance workshops that engage in contact with others are not designed to achieve any kind of absolute understanding or comprehension of others. Rather, these performance workshops strive to extend and amplify the ways we interact, and might interact, with others in order to appreciate and acknowledge the difference. Embodied reflexivity allows participants the opportunity to begin to account for the ways their actions, and understandings of others, always emerge in relationship to larger structures and systems. In the following section, we discuss the design of the performance workshop as a creative and critical practice of transformation.

PERFORMANCE WORKSHOP AS TRANSFORMATION

Not only can performance workshops be viewed as research, and contact, performance workshops can be defined as transformational. For us, the performance workshop functions as an exercise in critical pedagogy, which Kincheloe (2008) summarizes as, "the concern with transforming oppressive relations of power in a variety of domains that lead to human oppression" (p. 44). For us, critical pedagogy is a three-part practice. First, it requires an examination of what exists, particularly in educational contexts. Second, critical pedagogy necessitates locating power structures and systems that enable the status quo. Third, it demands that we create space for reimagining what justice and inclusivity entail. To engage in critical pedagogy means to engage with and examine particular phenomena (language, curricula, practices, etc.) to identify systems of power, and track how these systems of power grant certain privilege, access, and opportunities to particular groups and not others. Further critical pedagogy compels us to fervently pursue social justice by offering ways to intervene, interrupt, and change the status quo. Performance workshops can be designed and used as a form of critical pedagogy by working to explore, identify, and work toward changing oppressive systems and structures.

Within performance workshops, participants can develop an awareness of "what is" (i.e., the micro-practices and macrostructures that facilitate daily life), and then, through performance, participants can intervene in "what is" and reimagine what it could be. Therefore, we understand the performance workshop as a place in which transformation can begin to happen. Participants can performatively intervene in the status quo and generate new possibilities to enact social justice individually, relationally, and globally. In the subsequent section, we describe the transformative potential of the performance workshop through our own use of image work, drawing from Boal's (1992) image theater, in which performers are asked to create still embodied images of complex ideas, phenomenon, and/or specific happenings or events. The creation of these images then serves as a starting place for discussion, interpretation, and re-imagination of these ideas, phenomenon, or events.

We find image work particularly productive in a variety of contexts, for performers and non-performers, because the embodiment of an abstract idea or specific event requires participants to shift their focus from thinking to doing. Image work also enables participants to distill complex ideas, often larger than one body or individual, into manageable, tangible frames. For example, the abstract concept of "oppression" involves many bodies, and yet it affects individual bodies in specific and felt ways. In creating images, participants are able to begin to identify how these seemingly intricate and complicated ideas affect lived experience and the physical body. Finally, creating these images also creates the space for participants to imagine and experiment with alternative embodied configurations and responses to the concepts or events they are exploring. In a performance workshop, this move toward re-imagining and re-*imaging* functions as a starting place for transformation.

Image Work

When preparing a workshop that incorporates image work, we want participants to first gain some experience in creating, viewing and describing, and interpreting images. We often start by asking workshop participants to embody something that is familiar to them, like their own emotions or feelings. For instance, consider the following directions giving to participants in an initial image work session:

Taking your time walk, or move about in the space. Be aware of other bodies in motion, and try to fill the space as you move. Take note of how your feet hit the ground. Take note of your arms, and legs. Consider how you walk. Do you walk on your toes? On the balls of your feet? Take note of the speed at which you are walking. Continue to fill the space. Speed up. Move as if you feel rushed or hurried. Freeze in a hurried position. Take note of how your arms and legs positioned. Take note of any tension you feel in your body. Take note of where your head and face are positioned. Without moving too far out of your frozen position, look around the room. Notice how other bodies are positioned. What kinds of descriptive words would you use? As a group, try to describe body positioning of individual bodies and trends that you see without providing interpretations or evaluations of what positions might mean. As a group, from your descriptions, try to interpret what you have experienced.

Shake out your images. Let your bodies loosen up, and go back to moving about in the space. As you fill the space, try to perform how your body might react if you feel a headache coming on. Now freeze as if you have an intense headache. Take note of the positioning of your head, your facial expressions, your arms and legs. Now, as before, without moving from your position, notice the other bodies around you. As a group describe body positions. Drawing from your descriptions, try to make meanings from these still images.

Following this initial exercise, we ask workshop participants to develop images based on more complex or abstract ideas. For instance, in a workshop with new teachers, we ask participants to embody how they might feel walking into a classroom on the first day of class, as a first-time teacher. After creating these images, we ask the teachers to describe what they see in their own bodies and in the other teachers' bodies around them. Participants often describe: arms and legs held in at the body, exaggerated smiles, bodies miming holding on to a bag, books, binder, or other course materials. Whether prompted or not, participants usually interpret these images to mean that new teachers are excited, but nervous to be in the classroom.

In this same image work exercise, we ask new teachers to shift their perspective and to embody what it might be like to be a student. We ask them to remember their first day as a high school, university, or graduate student, and how they felt walking into a new classroom on the first day of class. In describing these images, workshop participants note how many students look expectant, tentative, or apathetic based on their amount of eye contact they offer. Participants describe body positions that render bodies as small as possible (i.e., arms and legs are held in). Participants also describe how "students" hold desks, books, a bag, etc. close to their bodies. Participants interpret the images of the first day for teachers and students in similar terms, especially regarding the feelings of anxiety and uncertainty.

In this workshop, new teachers begin to recognize similarities between their experiences as first-time teachers and the experiences their future students may face. When we have had enough time in the workshop, we have participants reimagine and re-perform their images as first-time teachers knowing their students might feel similarly nervous or anxious. These images are more relaxed; frequently, participants will include more open gestures to signal a welcome to students. In the past, participants have said that performing students not only offered insights into similar feelings of anxiety, but also allowed them to think about how they might be interpreting (or misinterpreting) student behavior, which then changes how they plan to approach the classroom. Even when there is not time to re-perform the first day as a teacher, participants' perspectives of that first day of classes shift, and they enter the classroom with insight they did not necessarily have before the workshop. In essence, these performance workshops offer the potential for transformation not only within the workshop, but also in their interactions and practices beyond the workshop.

Performing Change

Performance workshops that are specifically designed to enact a critical pedagogy, or a pedagogy that actively works to transform oppressive systems, may follow a variety of formats and address a range of concerns. Image work is only one way of working toward transformation in performance. Other possibilities, including the approaches previously mentioned for creating performance workshops for research and contact, may also be used in the service of working toward transformation or change. What is particularly significant about the practice of performance workshops as transformative is the emphasis on using performance to imagine alternative possibilities to the concepts, practices, or events that the workshop attempts to explore and understand.

The performance workshop as a practice of and for creating change follows the spirit of Dolan's (2005) discussion of utopia in performance. She articulates: "The very present-tenseness of performance lets audiences imagine utopia not as some idea of future perfection that might never arrive, but as brief enactments of the possibilities of a process that starts now, in this moment at the theater" (p. 17). For Dolan, performance opens the space for understanding, and even constituting, new configurations of reality. In terms of the performance workshop, the work of re-imagining and performing different possibilities also function as "enactments of the possibilities of a process that starts now" (p. 17). These performance workshops are a way of asking participants to begin actively working to create change.

ENGAGEMENT: CREATING A PERFORMANCE WORKSHOP

Engagement Description

The goal of this engagement is to provide you with a starting place for creating a performance workshop as form of conducting research. It is important to remember that there are a wide variety of performance methods, perspectives, and practices, and there are multiple different kinds of performance workshops that performance practitioners employ. However, it is still possible for somebody with limited performance experience to set up a session for engaging in inquiry through performance. In this section, we offer broad guidelines for creating a particular kind of workshop that asks participants to craft and present a staged performance of their research process and findings.

There are two factors to consider as you begin developing this particular kind of performance workshop: the kind of questions being posed, and the rules for experimentation. First, determine the kind of research that the performance workshop will address. For example, when teaching courses in communication and performance, we often create workshops aimed at understanding and exploring the topics in our classes. In a class on identity and culture, we might ask students to consider, in a workshop, how their identity is cultural or how their identity is constituted in/ by performance. By posing course topics as questions of *research*, students are invited to participate in the workshop as a generative learning process. You may also decide to design a workshop based on the individual research questions of the participants. In this case, it may be helpful to invite participants to develop these questions in advance of the workshop.

After determining the kind of research that participants will address, the second factor to consider in designing the workshop is the creation of the rules for experimentation and exploration. The goal of this workshop is for participants to engage in an embodied process of inquiry that results in the development of a presentation that demonstrates their research findings. Even if the research questions do not seem directly related to performance, it is still possible for participants to develop and present their findings in the form of a staged presentation/performance. In other words, performance functions, here, as a framework for testing and trying out the answers to a wide range of research questions. The format and expectations for the final presentation are used, in this example, as the starting place for developing the rules for experimentation and research throughout the workshop.

As you design the expectations for the final performance, develop instructions and rules that will enable a wide range of possible choices. Again, these rules do not necessarily need to be related to the research question, what is important is that the participants are given clear expectations for the design of the final presentation. Consider:

- How long will the final presentation be?
- What format will the presentation take? A dialogue? A monologue? A fully developed scene? A series of frozen images or tableau?
- Will the final performance involve more than one participant?
- Will you require the use of props?
- Will you require the use of gesture?
- Will you expect the use of repetition of text or movement?
- What will you expect in terms of vocal choices? Should there be a range of vocal variation (different volume, pitch, etc.)?
- What relationship will the performer create to or with the audience? Will the performer be expected to directly address the audience? Will the performer be expected to create a closed performance (no direct address to the audience)?

After establishing the expectations for the presentation, determine any additional rules or instructions for participants to follow during the development of their performances. This may include specific time for working on the presentation, specific rules for interacting with the other workshop participants, or other guidelines that may constrain or organize the ways participants interact and work toward the creation of their presentation. This use of rules offers what Bogart and Landau (2005) refer to as "a *sense* of order which, paradoxically, allows for more complexity and abandon inside the allotted time" (pp. 21–22). Creating an order, or structure for the workshop, can enable the generative and creative discoveries of the participants to emerge. The suggestions for structuring and organizing this particular workshop are offered as a starting place for creating the practice session of a performance workshop as a way of knowing, learning about, and working toward change in the world.

CLOSING

Performance workshops are practice sessions that are characterized by an emphasis on embodied knowing, the creation of new perspectives, and interaction with others. This practice session engages performance as a generative form or as a creative practice for bridging individual experiences and perspectives with broader cultural and social issues and concerns in three distinct ways. First, performance workshops enable a process of conducting research about human interaction and the world that emphasizes exploration, explanation, and that use exaggeration as a way of amplifying research findings. Second, performance workshops offer a way of engaging others through the consideration of the connection between the specific everyday practices of others and larger cultural and social systems and structures. Finally, performance workshops may be used as a practice for enacting and working toward change and social justice. As a pedagogical practice session, performance workshops provide a space for working with ideas, questioning the world, and imaging possibilities for change and new or better ways of interacting with others and the world.

REFERENCES

Alexander, B. K. (1998). Performing culture in the classroom: Excerpts from an instructional diary. In S. Dailey (Ed.), *The future of performance studies: Visions and revisions* (pp. 170–180). Annandale, VA: National Communication Association.

Alexander, B. K. (2000). *Skin Flint* (or, *The Garbage Man's Kid*): A generative autobiographical performance based on Tami Spry's *Tatoo Stories*. *Text and Performance Quarterly, 20,* 97–114.

Arnett, R. C. (2008). Provinciality and the face of the other: Levinas on communication ethics, terrorism—otherwise than originative agency. In K. Glenister Roberts & R. C. Arnett (Eds.), *Communication ethics: Between cosmopolitanism and provinciality.* (pp. 69–88). New York: Peter Lang.

Bell, E. (2008). *Theories of performance.* Thousand Oaks, CA: Sage.

Boal, A. (1979). *Theatre of the Oppressed.* (C. A. McBride & M. L. McBride, Trans.). New York: Theatre Communications Group (Original work published 1974).

Boal, A. (1992). *Games for actors and non-actors.* (A. Jackson, Trans). New York: Routledge.

Bogart, A. (2007). *And then, you act: Making art in an unpredictable world.* New York: Routledge.

Bogart, A., & Landau, T. (2005). *The viewpoints book: A practical guide to viewpoints and composition.* New York: Theatre Communications Group.

Bottoms, S., & Goulish, M. (Eds.). (2007). *Small acts of repair: Performance, ecology, and Goat Island.* New York: Routledge.

Bowman, M. S., & Bowman, R. L. (2002). Performing the mystory: A textshop in autoperformance. In N. Stucky & C. Wimmer (Eds.), *Teaching performance studies* (pp. 161–174). Carbondale: Southern Illinois University Press.

Conquergood, D. (1985). Performing as a moral act: Ethical dimensions of the ethnography of performance. *Literature in Performance, 5,* 1–13.

Dolan, J. (2005). *Utopia in performance: Finding hope at the theater.* Ann Arbor: University of Michigan Press.

Hall, S. (1985). Signification, representation, ideology: Althusser and the post-structuralist debates. *Critical Studies in Mass Communication, 2*(2), 91–114.

Huber, A., & McRae, C. (2014). Collaborative directing and teaching: Applications and extensions of critical performative pedagogy. *Departures in Critical Qualitative Research, 3*(3), 264–282.

Kincheloe, J. (2008). *Critical pedagogy primer* (2nd ed.). New York: Peter Lang.

Madison, D. S. (1999). Performing theory/embodied writing. *Text and Performance Quarterly, 19,* 107–124.

Pelias, R. J. (1999). *Writing performance: Poeticizing the researcher's body.* Carbondale, IL: Southern Illinois University Press.

Pelias, R. J., & Shaffer, T. S. (2007). *Performance studies: The interpretation of aesthetic texts* (2nd ed.). New York: Kendall Hunt.

Pineau, E. L. (1995). Re-Casting rehearsal: Making a case for production as research. *Journal of the Illinois Speech and Theatre Association, 46,* 43–52.

Spry, T. (2011). *Body, paper, stage: Writing and performing autoethnography.* Walnut Creek, CA: Left Coast Press.

Yordon, J. E. (1997). *Experimental theatre: Creating and staging texts.* Prospect Heights, IL: Waveland Press.

CHAPTER 4

Music and Routine

In this chapter, we present the musical practice session as a creative process that reveals insights about the function of routines and experimentation. This chapter offers an extended discussion of specific musical practices as generative forms of inquiry that can be used to extend critical approaches to pedagogy. Working from the example of our experiences learning and playing musical instruments, we use the context of our musical practice in order to develop and extend our arguments about the pedagogical and political functions of creativity. Musical experience or skill is not necessary for an appreciation or application of this session. Rather, this practice session opens the space for the recognition of how the design of routine and experimentation can work to critically recognize and engage larger structures, especially in pedagogical contexts. We argue music making can function as critical pedagogy in that it is culturally located and enacted on and by bodies (McRae 2015a, pp. 4–5) and therefore has the potential to highlight specific ways that cultural practices are (re)constituted by both musicians and audiences. As a creative act, music making can be further understood as critical pedagogy in that it is a site of embodied inquiry into the production of not only individual, but cultural, and social performances.

In addition to arguing for music making as critical pedagogy, we contend that making music emphasizes the cultivation of routine, which is necessary for understanding and facilitating critical pedagogy. For instance, routines function to organize and discipline bodies in order to accomplish particular practices, which may also maintain social and ideological structures. On the other hand, routines can also be developed to

© The Author(s) 2017   71
C. McRae and A. Huber, *Creating Performances for Teaching and Learning*,
Creativity, Education and the Arts, DOI 10.1007/978-3-319-54561-5_4

generate new practices that subvert and resist the status quo. To illustrate how music routines are developed, we describe the process of one of the authors continued practice of over twenty years of playing the trumpet, and of the other author's learning to play the ukulele. These musical practices offer an example of the pedagogical implications of the performances of learning through routine and experimentation.

Agenda

1. Warm-Up
2. Music making as critical pedagogy
3. Making music, making routine
4. Learning to play
5. Engagement: The listening instrument
6. Closing

WARM-UP

Tuning into Sound

This practice session begins with a warm-up that is particularly focused on sound and the act of listening. How do we encounter sounds? How do sounds saturate our experience? How do sounds shape our bodies? How do our bodies produce sounds? It is important to note that this focus on listening, like the emphasis on music and sound throughout this chapter, is not offered as an exclusionary practice. Though sound is often heard with and through the ear, we assume that listening may happen in a variety of different ways and with a range of sensory positions. Pedagogically this warm-up is offered as a starting place for considering and questioning the role of sound(s) in our lived experiences.

Take a deep breath.

Exhale.

Relax your shoulders.

What sounds surround you?

What are the first sounds you notice? Is there music playing on speakers in the room? Are there sounds coming from headphones you are wearing? Do you hear the murmur of voices? Is there laughter? Do you hear a baby crying? Do you hear sounds from a television or radio? Do you hear the sounds of animals? Do you hear birds chirping? Or dogs barking? Or a cat purring? What sounds are difficult to notice? Do you hear traffic? Is there construction nearby? Do you hear the sounds of machines? Do you hear the ticking of a clock? Do you hear the hum of an air conditioner or heater? Do you hear the whirring of a fan? Do you hear the faint buzzing of a light fixture? Do you hear fingers typing? Or pages turning? Do you hear the soft scratching of a pencil or pen writing on paper? What other sounds do you hear or feel? What noises constitute your current location?

Take a deep breath.

Exhale.

Relax your shoulders.

What sounds are you making?

How does your body sound in this space? What does it sound like when you breathe? Are you coughing, sniffling, or sneezing? What does it sound like when you yawn? Do you move your lips as you read? How do your movements sound? What does it sound like when you shift in your seat? How does it sound when you turn the pages of this book? How do your clothes sound when you move? Are you using any technological devices that sound? Do you have a watch that is ticking? Are you wearing glasses that sound when you stop to adjust their position on your face? Are you receiving vibrating messages on a phone? As you read are you taking part in any other tasks that also sound?

Take a deep breath.

Exhale.

Relax your shoulders.

What sounds linger?

What sounds remain with you? What sounds do you imagine? Do you hear the refrain of a popular song that is "stuck" in your head? Do you hear the parting words of a friend? Are you haunted by the words of a family member? Do you worry about the way you "sounded" in a previous interaction with a romantic partner? Can you "still hear" the laughter of the deceased?

Take a deep breath.

Exhale.

Relax your shoulders.

What sounds demand your attention?

Are there sounds that need to be repaired? Is there a squeaky door? Are there noises coming from your vehicle that need to be fixed? Do you hear alerts or alarms that indicate the time of important events or tasks? Are there sounds of discontent from colleagues that need your response? Are there sudden sounds that move your body to immediate action or reaction?

Take a deep breath.
Exhale.
Relax your shoulders.

Debriefing the Warm-up

Sounds permeate our spaces. Some sounds are immediately apparent and are emphasized by particular spaces. For example, in a concert hall the sounds and performances of an orchestra or band are often centered on a stage that an audience faces. Some sounds are less obvious and are even muted in some spaces. For example, the use of divider walls in office spaces work to separate the conversations and working sounds of the people in the space. Sounds also interact with and inform our practices. For example, the sound of music in some spaces might invite people to dance or even sing, whereas the subdued sounds of a library study room might invite practices that are equally restrained. The prompts in this warm-up are designed to draw attention to the role sound plays in our spaces and practices. These prompts are also offered as a starting place for thinking about the sensory practice of listening, and about the various ways we might practice listening as a pedagogical act and creative routine.

WARMING-UP AS ROUTINE

In reference to listening to various musical forms and genres, Stockfelt (1997) argues that listeners develop and employ different modes of listening. Different genres, contexts, and historical moments yield different listening practices (pp. 132–136). He goes on to suggest that listeners develop adequate modes of listening and explains:

> To listen adequately hence does not mean any particular, better, or "more musical," "more intellectual," or "culturally superior" way of listening. It means that one masters and develops the ability to listen for what is relevant to the genre in the music, for what is adequate to understanding according to the specific genre's comprehensible context. (p. 137)

In other words, an adequate mode of listening is a way of engaging particular musical genres according to the expectations and demands of that genre. This is similar to the ways audience members learn how to act and respond to various cultural performances like movies, theatrical productions, parades, or concerts. Kassabian (2002) extends and complicates the notion of adequate modes of listening with an argument for ubiquitous modes of listening. For Kassabian, a ubiquitous mode of listening is characterized by the ways listening to music is shaped by the pervasive sounds of music (pp. 135–141). In other words, listening to music is not so much a matter of genre; it is a matter of a practice that is ongoing and always happening.

Both adequate and ubiquitous modes of listening emphasize the process of listening to music as a culturally and contextually situated act. The prompts offered in this warm-up are a starting place for considering the ways our practices as listeners are similarly situated culturally and socially. Attending to the sounds we encounter and are surrounded by is a starting place for considering and recognizing the features and textures of our cultural context. The kinds of sounds we notice, the kinds of sounds we take-for-granted, the kinds of sounds we produce are all connected with and to larger cultural structures, social institutions, and political and historical contexts.

In addition to drawing attention to questions of context in terms of the sensory practice of listening, the prompts in this warm-up are also offered as a starting place for thinking about the individual practices and performances we enact as listeners. Like adequate and ubiquitous modes of listening, performative listening is offered as a way of characterizing the practice of listening (McRae 2015b, pp. 31–50). Performative listening is a theory of listening as a creative and constitutive performance of encountering and interacting with others (pp. 36–37). In other words, performative listening is a theory that suggests listening is a communicative act that creates realities and relationships. Thinking about and listening for the sounds we encounter, the sounds we produce, and the sounds that impact our daily lives is one strategy for beginning to consider our individual performance as listeners as a creative practice.

The particular focus of this warm-up activity on the sensory experience of sound is offered as one possible way of starting to identify the role context plays in shaping our individual sensory practices and performances. This activity also provides an opening for thinking about and questioning our individual practices and performances as listeners. How do we come to act as listeners? What worlds and relationships does our listening work to create? What sounds do we take-for-granted and why? What sounds do we notice and why? We are particularly interested in considering the ways our performances as listeners are always linked to larger cultural and contextual structures, as well as the ways we individually work to cultivate and develop particular performances as listeners. By questioning our individual practice as listeners, we can begin to think about how we create and might differently create our embodied responses and interactions with the world and others.

MUSIC MAKING AS CRITICAL PEDAGOGY

Music is always an act of performance. Small (1998) offers the term musicking as a way of describing music as an active process, and he explains: "To music is to take part, in any capacity, in a musical performance, whether by performing, by listening, by rehearsing or practicing, by providing material for performance (what is called composing), or by dancing" (p. 9). As a creative practice, musical performance is a process that is culturally located and is enacted by and on bodies (McRae 2015a, pp. 4–5). Throughout this section, musical performance, or musicking, is presented as a creative practice and critical pedagogy that includes the performances of both musicians and audience members. In other words, music performance is not limited to the practices of playing instruments or composing songs.

Music as a performance produced and engaged by musicians or audience members offers great pedagogical potential in terms of learning and thinking about the relationship between culture and embodiment. Cusick (1999) offers a clear argument regarding the link between bodies and music in terms of performances of gender:

> If bodily performances can be both constitutive *of* gender and metaphors
> *for* gender, then we who study the results of bodily performances like
> music might profitably look to our subject as a set of scripts for bodily per-
> formances which may actually constitute gender for the performers and
> which may be recognizable as metaphors of gender for those who witness
> the performers' displays. (pp. 14–15)

Music performance is a cultural act that might reveal and point to specific ways that cultural practices emerge and are (re)produced by musicians and audiences. McClary (1994) similarly identifies the importance of considering the embodied and cultural function of musical +performance (p. 78). Regarding the relationship between music and gender she asserts, "In other words, these issues are not 'extramusical;' they are inextricably bound up with musical procedures, procedures that have no value outside the social systems that produce and embrace them as somehow meaningful" (p. 71). The production of music is always linked to the maintenance and creation of particular social and cultural performances of identity that include gender, race, class, etc. (Holman Jones 1999; Shoemaker 2010; McRae 2010; Johnson 2002; Pineda 2009; Spry 2010; Koza 2008).

Music performance is produced by and generative of culture in ways that are always linked to bodies. As an example, Walser (1991) demonstrates the link between the social and cultural discourse about distortion and the significance of the sounds of a distorted electric guitar in particular as a marker of power. He explains, "To summarize, distortion is perceived as powerful in contemporary popular music because our socially-guided bodily experiences with distortion lead us to perceive it that way" (p. 125). In other words, musical sounds and practices (like distortion) are always enmeshed in cultural and social discourses. Therefore, music performance both participates in the creation of culture, and it is a practice that is always informed by ongoing social and cultural practices.

This discussion of music as an active process that is always interconnected with cultural and social identities, practices, and values offers an opening for considering the critical pedagogical possibilities of music. Music performance, as a creative act, can be understood as critical pedagogy in at least two distinct ways: first, as a site of inquiry regarding the embodied production of cultural and social performances and second as an embodied practice and way of learning.

The first way music performance is generative for the development of a critical pedagogy is as an embodied site of inquiry regarding the functions and implications of social and cultural performances. As an esthetic form, music performance exemplifies the connections between larger structures and individual practices. Langer's (1953) description of music as a significant form helps clarify this link:

> The basic concept is the articulate but non-discursive form having import without conventional reference, and therefore presenting itself not as a symbol in the ordinary sense, but as a "significant form," in which the factor of significance is not logically discriminated, but is felt as a quality rather than recognized as a function. (p. 32)

In other words, music comes to be meaningful through its form. Music does not simply represent concepts, but it is an experience. In terms of critical pedagogy, the production and reception of music is a demonstration, and sounding, of sociocultural beliefs, values, and practices. Music, as a significant form, is an important starting place for thinking about and investigating the ways social and cultural practices take shape and are (re)produced. Music teaches, produces, and maintains particular cultural values, systems, and relationships.

In addition to the function of music performance as an example and demonstration of cultural formations, music also presents a creative act, and embodied way of learning, that can be a critical pedagogy. In other words, the creative process and practice of making music (as audience or musician) can work as a critical pedagogical act. In particular, the routine of learning to produce music presents an embodied process of generating knowledge that can aid in the development of critical pedagogical processes of learning. Warren (1999) refers to this critical embodied way of learning as a performative pedagogy (p. 258). For Warren, performative pedagogy features both a performative mode of analysis and a performative mode of engagement. He explains:

> A performative pedagogy of enfleshment promotes a performative mode of analysis—a study of how human beings constitute the embodied practices of their daily lives. Performative pedagogy also features a performative mode of engagement—a methodology of engaging in education that acknowledges bodies and the political nature of their presence in our classrooms. (p. 258)

Performative pedagogy, and the modes of analysis and engagement presented by Warren, indicates the possibilities of learning to create music as an act of critical pedagogy. In particular, performative modes of analysis and engagement work to reflexively acknowledge the ways embodied practices, like music making, constitute experiences in ways that are always cultural and political.

These approaches to music as critical pedagogy work to engage and consider the following kinds of questions: How do we learn to produce music (as musicians or audience members)? How is this production of music cultural? What social values shape the practice of learning to produce or listen to music? How do musical experiences challenge social and cultural performances of identity? How does the production of music present the opportunity for creating new cultural practices and performances?

In the following sections, we discuss our experiences learning to create music as an example of the ways music functions as an act of critical pedagogy. We focus on two aspects of music making as critical pedagogy: routine and learning to play new instruments. In these sections, we propose strategies for engaging in music making practices that include playing musical instruments and listening to music.

MAKING MUSIC, MAKING ROUTINE

I open the latches on the hard shell case and am greeted with the familiar sight and smells of the inside of my trumpet case. The crushed velvet fabric cradles the trumpet, and the smell of petroleum from the valve oil sticks in the air. I pick the horn up with my left hand and gently set the mouthpiece into the lead pipe. Standing with my feet shoulder width apart, I bring the trumpet to my lips. I adjust my posture, correcting for my tendency to lean back on my hips. Without taking the horn off of my lips, I inhale from the corners of my mouth and begin the slight buzzing of my lips in order to produce my first note of the day. I listen to the ways the tone wavers in and out of pitch as I continue playing this single note. I make adjustments to the muscles in my embouchure until I can hold an unwavering tone for more than a few seconds. I press the second valve down on the horn and play the next note, again working for a steady stone. I continue this exercise, playing down the scale in long tones, and then, I set the trumpet down in order to rest the muscles in my lips.

While resting my lips, I set up my wire music stand where I place a book of technical exercises for trumpet. I open to a page with lines of music that is dog-eared and covered in pencil markings. This is the same page I played from every day for the last week. I set my digital metronome on the stand and set the tempo to click 120 beats per min. The high-pitched staccato ticking of the metronome creates a consistent and persistent soundtrack for the remainder of the practice session. I pick up my trumpet, again in my left hand, and place the mouthpiece against my lips. I inhale from the corners of my mouth and begin pushing the valves down to correspond with the notes on the page and the clicking tempo of the metronome. The exercise is only three lines long, and it takes less than a minute to play. After the line ends, I rest for the same amount of time as I played. Then, I move on to the next passage of music.

After playing several passages in the book of technical studies, I set a binder of songs that I am working to learn and memorize. The songs are mostly jazz standards like "My Funny Valentine," "All of Me," and "Moonlight Becomes You." I spend a few minutes playing each song, following the notes written on the page, and then I repeat each song several times in different keys. I end the practice session by trying to play, from memory, the songs I am working on that day.

Discipline and Routine

The musical routine described above is one way Chris organizes his musical practice sessions when playing the trumpet. The organized set of procedures, from the specific movements of his body to the exercises and songs he plays, function as a practice of disciplining of the body that engenders a specific kind of creative learning. What this kind of deliberate structure for playing music enables, and can reveal about creative practices as critical pedagogy, is a learning process that emphasizes embodiment, repetition, and reflection.

Playing the trumpet entails certain physical factors including breath control and the strengthening of the muscles in the embouchure. In the routine described above, certain practices, like the playing of long tones (playing and holding single notes for long periods of time in a single breath), are deliberately and directly centered on developing these physical abilities. The repetition of playing these long tones at the beginning of every practice session works to improve and maintain the breath and muscle control needed for playing the trumpet. Finally, playing long tones is not only a matter of developing physical capacities through repeated action, this practice also entails reflection. While holding the notes, and after playing the notes, adjustments are made for improvement and refinement.

This routine for practice accounts for and attends to the embodied requirements of playing the trumpet. Sudnow's (1993) ethnomethodological discussion of learning to play jazz piano exemplifies this when he says, "Every musical style as the creation of human bodies entails correspondingly constituted tactile facilities for its performers" (p. 13). Practicing music in this way disciplines and normalizes particular embodied acts and actions. The routine for learning and practicing a musical instrument is a disciplining or creation of bodies and facilities. The function of a musical routine to discipline bodies also points to the ways other routines may also structure and organize bodies in the service of particular outcomes and goals. Identifying routines as particular pedagogical practices (in a variety of contexts, not limited to musical practices), describing and detailing the processes of routines, and questioning and analyzing the roles of routines in shaping bodies can begin to link individual practices and habits to larger cultural values (McLaren 1999; Willis 1981; Warren 2003).

The example of the musical routine presents an opening for deliberately generating and designing routines as part of a creative and critical pedagogy. For example, routines may be designed to discipline and organize bodies in ways that acknowledge and value differences. As Pineau (2002) argues, "Through deliberate, arduous, and consistent effort, bodies can acquire a new way of being" (p. 45). Routines are practices for generating new ways of being; however, not all routines work in the service of critical pedagogy, or of transforming oppressive structures and systems. What can be learned from the musical routine, and applied to other classroom contexts, is the focus on deliberate and even minute tasks that can be embodied, repeated, and refined through reflection. Routines are starting places for future actions. For example, if a broad goal of critical pedagogy is to revise oppressive structures, then a routine that engenders a space for conversation and interaction amongst students could be a starting place for this kind of project.

The musical routine provides an example of the function and form of routines that might be used as a starting place for critical examination of pedagogical routines in a wide variety of contexts. Musical routines also serve as an analogy for the development of other routines in critical pedagogy in terms of the organized and intentional structure that emphasize embodiment, repetition, and reflection. Routines offer an important pedagogical function in creative practices. In addition to marking the importance of routines through the example of musical practices, it is also important to consider the fact that these particular routines are designed in the service of producing and music. In the following section, we discuss the relationship between esthetic production and routines as an act of critical pedagogy.

Esthetic Production and Routine

Over time, the long tones sound even and unwavering. Over time, the technical exercises are played without hesitation or error. Over time, the binder with jazz standards loses its structural integrity. The pages of songs become wrinkled, and even torn. The need to follow the notes on the page decreases, as the time spent practicing increases. Musical patterns are memorized, and new possibilities for playing with the structures and melodies emerge. Over time, the routine enables and improves musical performance and production.

Routines can be created and implemented in the service of a variety of practices with a variety of generative effects. For example, routines for creative practices may be implemented in order to improve those practices (practicing the trumpet in order to sound and play better), but they may also be engaged in order to produce a particular way of thinking and knowing (practicing trumpet in order to think about musical structures and relationships differently). Regarding the pedagogical value of her experience as a dancer, Stinson (1995) explains, "Yet it is the lived experience of dancing that I have found to be most influential in my thinking and writing, and which has provided the metaphors that have helped me to understand my life and my work as a scholar" (p. 43). Stinson's experience as a dancer worked to shape, not only her specific embodied practice of dancing, but it also shaped her ways of being and knowing. Extending and applying a musical routine as critical pedagogy emphasizes the generative possibilities of music as a creative practice and way of being and knowing.

Considering music as an active process that is made through a variety of activities including playing instruments, singing, and listening allows for the possibility of enacting musical routines regardless of any specific musical talent. The ability to engage with music is the only prerequisite for developing a musical routine. So, for example, musical routines are not limited to vocal warm-ups or technical exercises on instruments, but could include practices of listening and engaging music as audience member. What a musical routine that centers on a musical practice (like listening) might offer critical pedagogy is an emphasis on embodiment and a musically structured approach to learning and interacting with others.

Musical routines are distinctly embodied practices. As DeChaine (2002) explains, "The body offers itself up *in collaboration* with sound in the production of the musical text. In this way it functions as both performer and instrument" (p. 83). Regardless of the kind of music being played, or musical practice being engaged, bodies are always implicated. Therefore developing a musical routine aids in the development of a bodily awareness. In terms of critical pedagogy, the musical routine emphasizes the ways learning shapes and is shaped by the body.

Musical routines are also always linked with the reception and production of sound. The sensory experience of sound presents a way of thinking and learning that emphasizes relationships and differences in ways that are distinctly different from other modes of learning (Bresler 2008; McRae and Nainby 2015). Not only does music draw attention to the actions of others, musical acts also present opportunities for self-reflection and awareness. Kun (2005) explains:

> When you hear it, music makes you immediately conscious of your identity precisely because something outside of you is entering your body—alien sounds and frequency, the very bones and tissues of your being. All musical listening is a form of confrontation, of encounter, of the meeting of worlds and meanings, when identity is made self-aware and is, therefore, menaced through its own interrogation. (p. 13)

Listening to or producing musical sounds presents a learning opportunity that features interaction, individual perception, and difference. The encounter with musical sounds does not necessarily result in a foregone conclusion of meaning, but it does present an opportunity for experiencing new and different relationships and structures.

Monson (2007) presents the concept of perceptual agency in terms of listening to music, to describe the practice of shifting attention to various aspects of a musical performance including rhythms, harmonies, melodies, etc. (p. s39). This change in focusing on the listener results in different understandings of and recognitions about a particular musical performance. For example, focusing on the sounds of a particular instrument (like the trumpet) results in a different experience of a musical performance, then if a listener were to focus on another instrument (like the drums or piano). As a generative characteristic of listening, perceptual agency works toward understandings of events and interactions as multiple and always interconnected. Musical practices, like listening, offer both an embodied way of engaging music, and practicing a critical pedagogy that values difference and works to account for the role of the self.

Designing Routine

A routine of engaging and practicing music shapes an embodied way of being, and it shapes the ways music is produced and encountered. In order to design a musical routine as a kind of critical act that is not limited by access to musical instruments, or a particular expertise with musical notation, developing a listening routine may be a productive starting place. The following listening routine is offered as a generic example of the ways listening might be practiced as a creative act that emphasizes embodied learning and purposeful self-reflection. Other more specific approaches and ways of listening to music exist. This routine may be followed individually, or these steps could be used for leading a small group or class.

First, prepare and move to a listening space. This space does not need any particular unique features, but it does need to be distinct from other spaces. For example, if this routine takes place in a classroom, the listening space should be distinct from the location of the daily instruction and discussion. A listening space could be established by simply reconfiguring the relationship of bodies in the classroom. Ideally, for future iterations of this routine, the configuration of space would be consistent.

Second, breathe deeply. Focus on the act of breathing. Notice how your body breathes. Notice the parts of your body that move as you breathe. Notice any sounds your body makes as you continue to breathe.

Third, shift your focus from breathing to engaging the sounds and vibrations that fill the space around you. Begin by attending to, and noticing, the sounds that are closest to you or produced by you. Then, attend to the sounds directly to your left, to your right, above you, below you, in front of you, and finally behind you.

Fourth, engage a musical example or recording. This example may be played on any device, and it may follow any kind of genre. As you encounter this recording for the first time, take note of the musical feature you notice first. Pay attention to the way your body responds or reacts to this music. Then, focus your attention on a particular characteristic of this recorded performance. For example, try to follow the sounds of the drums or percussion instruments. Play the song one more time, and again attend to the sounds of the same specific musical characteristic.

Finally, in order for this exercise to take shape *as* a routine it is important to follow this process in a consistent manner over a period of several days. The design of the routine should stay the same, though additional steps may be added, and different musical examples may be incorporated or substituted.

LEARNING TO PLAY

The instrument looks familiar, but feels strange. I took violin lessons as a child, but stopped playing in fifth grade when I showed aptitude for the trumpet and was chosen for band, not orchestra. The ukulele is not entirely unlike the shape and weight of the ¾ violin I played, but neither is it the same. Holding this lightweight acoustic instrument feels peculiar. It seems lighter somehow, as if the agathis wood does not carry the same gravitas as my little maple violin. Maybe it's a Western bias where the violin is part of every classical orchestra, or perhaps it's in my own reasons for learning to play the violin and the ukulele.

Learning the violin I wanted to emulate the great grandfather I never knew but heard of often, by bringing life back to his old fiddle. My motivation for learning the ukulele is somewhat different. I have no need to live up to anyone, nor does anyone I know play the ukulele. Perhaps this novelty is even part of why I have chosen it, so that no one has expectations for my playing. I want to learn the ukulele to contribute to my family who loves music, not by playing the trumpet, drums, bass, or guitar, all instruments which my partner is already proficient, but by playing something all of my own. I want to learn this instrument so, like my partner, I too can pick out simple tunes to play and sing for our children when we're together as a family. I like the ukulele because it has little pretense, it is small enough to pack up to take to the beach, and it is quiet enough that I can bring it to my office or public and play for myself without disturbing others.

I cradle the hollow wooden instrument in my arms, I support the neck with my left hand and I rest my fingers of my right hand on the four nylon strings. I brush my thumb across the strings and realize I have no idea of where to begin. Unlike the violin, played with a bow, the ukulele requires me to strum notes. I had thought that strumming would sort of just come to me, and yet as I sit down to play I realize there's a lot more to it than I first believed.

I strum down multiple times. It doesn't sound quite right to me. Then I strum down and up. This pattern sounds more like what I was expecting, but still isn't exactly it. I thumb through the pages of the beginner's ukulele book my partner has given me. The author discusses different strumming patterns; they are marked on a musical staff as little hash marks, noting when to strum "down" and "up." There are several patterns: strumming down, strumming down, up, down, up, strumming down, down, up, down, down. This is confusing for me. I cannot hear what these patterns are supposed to sound like.

Over the next few weeks, I begin developing a routine for playing the ukulele. Since I am not taking formal lessons, my approach to learning the ukulele is mostly through trial and error. In addition to struggling through my beginner's books, I download a ukulele station on my computer so I can listen to the music when I am not practicing. I also look up instructional videos for beginners on the Internet, which I watch, re-watch, and play along until my technique, strumming patterns, and chords start to resemble what I hear. I surf the web for major and minor ukulele chords and diagrams, sketching them in my daily journal so that I can refer back to them during rehearsal. I rely most on my partner to listen to what I have learned and ask questions about what my Internet teachers have said about technique, strumming patterns and chords. Since he plays the guitar, he is able to answer most of my questions about playing the ukulele, which has many parallels to the string instrument he already knows.

Each day for weeks, I spend time looking up or reviewing strategies and methods for playing the ukulele, and 20–30 min practicing chords, chord progressions, alternating strumming patterns. As I study, rehearse, and repeat, I notice particular changes to my body from the way I hold the instrument while sitting, to the preference I develop to strum with the right thumb, to the calluses on my left fingertips from playing chords over and over. As I practice, my fingers begin to move faster amongst chord progressions and my strumming patterns become less awkward. I am finding myself thinking less about each part of my playing and more time focusing on the songs I am trying to play. Practicing doesn't make me less of a novice, but it allows me to experiment more.

Privilege and Experimentation

This account of learning to play the ukulele reveals Aubrey's practice of musical experimentation and discovery. Learning to play a musical instrument is an embodied practice of learning that foregrounds and features mistakes, barriers, reflection, and production. As a creative process, learning to play a new musical instrument can also inform a critical pedagogy. Not only does the practice of learning to play musical instruments reveal important insights about the way privilege shapes education, this practice also emphasizes the value of privileging experimental modes of learning.

In educational contexts, playing music is not immune to cultural and institutional systems that produce and participate in the maintenance of various forms of privilege, or unearned advantage. Koza (2008) offers an example of the ways university school of music vocal auditions "systematically advantage some applicants while disadvantaging others" (p. 145). In particular, these auditions work to privilege vocal performances that are linked to class and race (pp. 146–150). First, access to private lessons, and the kinds of training and technical proficiency provided by these lessons, is privileged during the auditions. Second, these auditions value performances of an exclusive repertoire of European and classical musical compositions. Koza's observations point to the ways these particular vocal auditions maintain the privilege of whiteness, but these observations also emphasize the ways musical performances participate in the production and maintenance of cultural systems (including cultural forms of privilege). Music performances are cultural practices that are always linked to the production of cultural values and systems.

Even in a non-competitive framework, learning to play a musical instrument relies on various forms of cultural privilege. Access to new instruments, instructional materials, and the time for experimentation and explorations are all notable and necessary privileges. Who can afford different instruments? Who has access to learning materials or teachers? Who has time to experiment? Attending to these advantages is an attempt to reflexively consider the ways individual creative practices are always shaped by larger cultural structures and systems (McRae 2015b, p. 57). Accounting for the various ways our modes of learning and experimentation are enabled and constrained is a process that can lead not only to recognition of privilege, but also to the development of new opportunities and possibilities.

Creative educational practices, like learning to play a new musical instrument, are acts that can reveal privilege, but these practices also demonstrate the value of privileging experimental modes of learning. The privilege of learning to play a new instrument also presents valuable opportunities for learning that centers on mistakes, challenging obstacles, self-reflection, and generative production. This is a creative practice that might enable new ways of knowing and being in the world and with others.

Harris (2014) warns against the increasing call for creativity and innovation in education that appears as a form of marketable skill. She explains:

Yet the conflation of creativity with innovation is a form of ideological gentrification, in that while appearing to value the arts and creative endeavour

it is really redirecting and narrowing the discourse of creativity into productive innovation and marketplace measures of value. And this more than
anything signals the death knell of 'arts education,' which remains tainted
by its relationship to risk, un-productivity (time-wasting, daydreaming)
and 'failure'—all of which are increasingly impossible in a marketplace
economy. (p. 19)

Creativity and creative approaches to learning are often engaged and
supported in and by educational institutions in the service of developing
a marketable talent. For Harris, this undermines the non-commodifiable
qualities of creativity that include risk taking, daydreaming, and wasting
time. Harris explains, "Arts education advocates argue that vital to this
creative process are such under-valued and increasingly outlawed activities as daydreaming, provoking, brainstorming and commemorating, and
sometimes failing miserably in the conceptual endeavour attempted" (p.
18). The attempts to convert creativity into a vocational skill weaken the
possibility and potential of creativity as a generative way of learning and
being.

What might a non-marketable approach to creativity as an educational
practice look like? And how does the example of learning to play a musical instrument provide awareness about what might be most valuable
about a creative learning process? Taking the time to explore and learn
a new instrument might offer new metaphors and frameworks for understanding relationships and difference. Playing a new instrument might
also reveal broad insights about time, rhythm, and harmony. There may
be countless lessons and revelations that emerge in the creative process
of experimenting with a new instrument. One of the most important and
specific lessons of this particular creative practice is regarding the body of
the student.

Bodies and/as Instruments

Over time, the shape and weight of the ukulele may start to feel comfortable. The texture of the nylon strings may seem more familiar. However,
the instrument may not be fully understood. The need to consciously
think about where and how to place fingers on the strings may decrease,
but the need to stop and think may still be there. The strumming patterns may become progressively easier to play, but the feel of this new
practice may still seem strange. Learning the techniques for playing a

new instrument is a gradual process that reveals how the body learns and how the body shapes and is shaped by the instrument.

Experimenting with and exploring a new musical instrument functions as a creative and critical pedagogy that emphasizes the central role of the body as a site of learning. First, playing a new instrument draws attention to the body. Leder (1990) presents a phenomenological account of the ways our bodies disappear from our attention. He gives as an example, the "background disappearance" of his legs when he is sitting (p. 27). His legs are still a part of his body, but his attention is drawn away from the legs in a way that allows his legs to become absent or to disappear. Leder then extends this discussion of disappearance to technologies, and he argues technologies can undergo the same disappearance as parts of the body. He says, "I live in bodies beyond bodies, clothes, furniture, room, house, city, recapitulating in ever expanding circles aspects of my corporeality. As such, it is not simply my surface organs that disappear but entire regions of the world with which I dwell in intimacy" (p. 35). The perceived disappearance or absence of bodies, technologies, and environments is not necessarily good or bad, but it is indicative of taken-for-granted practices.

Drawing attention to taken-for-granted practices and embodied performances can yield a critical awareness of the ways, even the most seemingly mundane acts, are always linked to history and culture. Or as Butler (1988) explains regarding gender, the performances of our bodies are always a result of "sedimented acts" (p. 523). In other words, our embodied ways of accomplishing gender are always situated historically and culturally. Practices that ask us to engage in the use of our bodies in new or unfamiliar ways can begin to reveal the aspects of our bodies that are taken-for-granted or seemingly absent.

Learning to play a new musical instrument, for example, is a practice that requires the use of the body in new ways. This new practice and new embodied mode of learning can draw awareness and attention back to the body as central to the process of learning. The questions that are raised about the body by learning to interact with and engage a new instrument can lead to an awareness and reflexivity about learning as an embodied act. In addition to drawing attention to and awareness about the body, learning a new musical instrument also points to the intra-active relationship between technologies and bodies (Barad 2007, p. 139).

Peters (2015) explains the relationship between technology and humans as one that is always already intertwined and interconnected (p. 88–90). In other words, humans are not separable from technologies. He explains:

> The fear of "technological determinism" serves to uphold a barrier between mind and matter, human and thing, animal and machine, art and nature—precisely the continuities across which the most interesting cultural histories of media are written. By isolating acute parts of our world as technology that we should control, it effaces the existential fact that we live environmentally, dependently, in apparatuses not of our own making, starting with the womb itself. (p. 89)

For Peters, humans and technologies are co-constituting, and never entirely separable entities (p. 90). Technologies shape and are shaped by humans. The ukulele shapes and is shaped by Aubrey. What is important about learning to play a new instrument is not the discrete role of the performer and the instrument, rather what is significant is the dynamic interaction between performer and instrument that emerges.

Gingrich-Philbrook and Simmons (2015) pose a similar argument in their call for a posthumanist theory of the relationship between performers and technology that moves away from a utilitarian view of technology (p. 328). If the value of technology is not a question of use or usefulness, then a consideration of the dynamic interaction between technologies and bodies becomes possible. In other words, rather than asking: what is the educational use of learning a new musical instrument? Or, what does learning to play the ukulele add to an education? The question that learning a new musical instrument poses is: what kinds of educational possibilities are constituted by this new interaction? Or, what possibilities for learning are engendered by playing the ukulele? Learning to play the ukulele, or learning to play any new musical instrument, creates possibilities for new educational interactions that may or may not be linked explicitly to the musical instrument.

In the case of Aubrey's learning to play the ukulele, the emergent educational possibilities are not necessarily about doing something productive, or moving toward a fixed goal, or achieving a set learning outcome. Instead learning this musical instrument is pedagogically generative of play and sensory interaction with others. Learning a new instrument creates possibilities for failures *and* discoveries that may or may not pertain to music, the body, culture, privilege, difference, inter-action, routine, or something else altogether.

Exploring and Playing

Learning to play a new instrument is always an act of privilege and access. Raising the question of who can afford the time, materials, and space for creating music should not be avoided. Valuing experimentation and the kind of learning that exploring and learning a new instrument engenders does not need to be limited to the procurement of musical instruments per se. For example, new instruments that may be used for the creation of music may include found objects, use of movement, or use of voice. The following prompts are offered as one possible start-ing place for creating a practice that privileges musical exploration and experimentation as a critical creative act.

First, gather materials for creating music. This may include an instru-ment, but it may also include household objects (pots, pans, kitchen utensils, electronic devices, toys, office supplies, tools, papers, containers, etc.). Discovering items for making music is not necessarily a question of identifying culturally recognized musical instruments that are available for purchase. Rather, finding instruments for making music is a question of expanding the notion of what might be considered musical.

Second, explore the capacity of this new instrument for producing sounds. What sounds are possible to produce through your interaction with the instrument? Can you make loud sounds? Can you make quiet sounds? Can you make sounds quickly? Can you make sounds slowly? Can you make sounds that are short in duration? Can you make sounds that are sustained? The question of exploring and experimenting with musical instruments is not necessarily: How can I play this particular instrument correctly? Rather, the question is: How can I interact with this instrument?

Third, as you discover the limits of this instrument and your abilities for interaction with the instrument select two or three sounds that you can replicate. Try to repeat these sounds several times. Pay specific atten-tion to your movements. How do you hold the instrument? How do you hold your body? How are you breathing? What inconsistencies do you notice as you repeat each sound? What consistencies do you notice?

Continue exploring the possibilities of this instrument. What new sounds become possible as you continue playing? What do you notice about your own choices, movements, and style of interacting with this instrument? This process of exploring and experimenting with the production of sound, even in ways that may not be immediately and culturally be recognized as musical, is one way of attending to the ways the body learns and accounting for the pedagogical value of musical exploration.

ENGAGEMENT: THE LISTENING INSTRUMENT

Engagement Description

The goal of this engagement is to offer a musical practice session that may be extended to pedagogical contexts, like the classroom, in order to question and consider the ways learning is always an embodied and exploratory act. Working from the exercises offered earlier in this chapter for designing routines and experimenting with the production of sound, this engagement focuses specifically on listening as a musical and embodied act. In this section, we provide guidelines for staging a practice session that features a routine of creating and reproducing sounds.

Begin by asking participants to bring, or find, objects that may be used for creating sounds. Ideally, these objects should be mundane, readily available, and not necessarily musical objects/instruments. The request for instruments may be adjusted with a variety of parameters. For example, participants may be asked to bring an instrument from a specific room of their house (the kitchen, the bathroom, the living room, etc.). Other parameters may include specific qualities or characteristics including functions (electronic/non-electronic, decorative, structural), material (made of paper, plastic, metal, glass, etc.) or size (handheld, fits in a bag, weighs less than a dictionary, etc.). Offering specific guidelines for finding an instrument can help narrow the search, and it can also help participants identify taken-for-granted objects as possible instruments.

Once the participants of the session are prepared with their instruments, provide time for experimentation and exploration of the range of possible sounds. What are the possible for creating sounds with the object? How many different sounds are possible? After the initial exploration with the instrument ask participants to focus on the following three characteristics of sound: volume, duration, and tempo. First, ask participants to generate sounds in a range of volumes from soft to loud. Then, ask the participants to play with duration in creating sounds. What is the longest sound that can be made? What is the shortest sound that can be created? Finally, ask participants to experiment with different tempos as they play their found instruments.

Next, ask the participants to compose a fifteen-second-long repeatable pattern of sounds on their instruments. Instruct the participants to attend to and vary their use of volume, duration, and tempo in their compositions. Each sound within the sequence should be clearly definable in terms of these three qualities (volume, duration, and tempo). Ask participants to practice and repeat these newly created patterns three times, each time working for greater consistency.

After creating and practicing the new composition ask the participants to pair with one another and to share their compositions. Then, ask the participants to share the composition a second time. After the second performance, ask the listening partner to repeat or play back the pattern on their found instrument. At this point in the engagement the process can be repeated, the partners may provide each other with instructions for repeating the composition, or a broader discussion and debriefing of the engagement may take place amongst all of the participants.

In order to avoid evaluative commentary on the quality of the sounds produced and reproduced by the participants, a discussion about the activity should focus on detailed descriptions of and reflections on the experience. For example, participants may be asked to discuss and answer the following kinds of questions:

- What were the challenges of creating sounds on the found object?
- What did you discover as you played the instrument?
- How did you produce different volumes, durations, and tempos of sound?
- What did you learn about your instrument when you attempted to create a fifteen-second composition?
- What happened to the composition as you worked to repeat the patterns?
- How did the composition change when you performed for a partner?
- What were the challenges of listening to these compositions?
- What happened when you tried to reproduce the composition created by your partner?

The process of and discussion about playing, listening to, and reproducing sounds on these found objects/instruments is designed as a starting place for engaging ideas about learning through routines and exploration. This engagement also works to privilege and feature embodied and experimental creative practices.

Closing

Music is a creative practice and performance that is always linked to questions of culture and embodiment. Definitions and evaluations of music are always culturally located, and the production of music (either through the interaction with instruments, or by the act of listening) is always enabled and constrained by specific bodies. This practice session engages music as a generative pedagogical form in terms of routine and experimental and exploratory modes of learning. The routines of learning to play and practice music work to organize and structure embodied modes of performance, and these routines also engender the creation of an esthetic form. The function of musical routines might be analogously extended to other pedagogical practices as a demonsstration of the ways routines might function to enable creative possibilities. However, musical routines are also pedagogically valuable for their unique sensory focus on the production and reception of sound. A routine of listening and reflecting on the ways sounds are made by particular bodies could be the starting place of a mode of engaging others that is critical, reflexive, and empathetic (McRae 2015b).

In addition to the pedagogical value of routines, this practice session also considers the critical and pedagogical implications of learning to play a new musical instrument. Exploring a new instrument reveals and points to the privileges of access and time that creative practices often require. In addition to awareness of privilege, this practice also points to the pedagogical and critical value of privileging experimentation. In this way, learning (regardless of successfulness) to play a new musical instrument presents countless opportunities and openings for self-awareness, reflexivity, and the development of new perspectives.

Finally, as part of a pedagogical practice session, music performances provide a space for engaging in routines and processes of experimentation that privileges listening as a critical mode of learning from and engaging others. Listening, as a characteristic of musical performance, is a creative act that also works toward a critical pedagogy that values an open engagement with others. Creating routines and experimental opportunities with music may reveal a range of pedagogical opportunities; and of these, the opportunity for rethinking and refining the practice of listening is of central importance.

REFERENCES

Barad, K. (2007). *Meeting the universe halfway: Quantum physics and the entanglement of matter and meaning*. Durham: Duke University Press.

Bresler, L. (2008). The music lesson. In J. G. Knowles & A. L. Cole (Eds.), *Handbook of the arts in qualitative research* (pp. 225–237). Thousand Oaks, CA: SAGE.

Butler, J. (1988). Performative acts and gender constitution: An essay in phenomenology and feminist theory. *Theatre Journal, 40*, 519–531.

Cusick, S. G. (1999). Gender, musicology, and feminism. In N. Cook & M. Everist (Eds.), *Rethinking music* (pp. 471–498). Oxford: Oxford University Press.

DeChaine, D. R. (2002). Affect and embodied understanding in musical experience. *Text and Performance Quarterly, 22*, 79–98.

Gingrich-Philbrook, C., & Simmons, J. (2015). Reprogramming the stage: A heuristic for posthuman performance. *Text and Performance Quarterly, 35*, 323–344.

Harris, A. (2014). *The creative turn: Toward a new aesthetic imaginary*. Rotterdam: Sense.

Holman Jones, S. (1999). Women, musics, bodies, and texts: The gesture of women's music. *Text and Performance Quarterly, 19*, 217–235.

Johnson, E. P. (2002). Performing blackness down under: The Café of the Gate of Salvation. *Text and Performance Quarterly, 22*(2), 99–119.

Kassabian, A. (2002). Ubiquitous listening. In D. Hesmondhalgh & K. Negus (Eds.), *Popular music studies* (pp. 131–142). London: Oxford University.

Koza, J. E. (2008). Listening for whiteness: Hearing racial politics in undergraduate school music. *Philosophy of Music Education Review, 16*, 145–155.

Kun, J. (2005). *Audiotopia: Music, race, and America*. Berkeley, CA: University of California.

Langer, S. K. (1953). *Feeling and form*. New York: Charles Scribner's Sons.

Leder, D. (1990). *The absent body*. Chicago: The University of Chicago.

McClary, S. (1994). Paradigm dissonances: Music theory, cultural studies, feminist criticism. *Perspectives of New Music, 32*(1), 68–85.

McLaren, P. (1999). *Schooling as ritual performance: Toward a political economy of educational symbols and gestures (3rd ed.)*. New York, NY: Rowman & Littlefield Publishers. (Original work published 1986).

McRae, C. (2010). Singing I Will Survive: Performance as evolving relationship. *Cultural Studies <=>Critical Methodologies, 10*(4), 326–333.

McRae, C. (2015a). Hearing performance as music. *Liminalities: A Journal of Performance Studies, 11*(5), 1–19.

McRae, C. (2015b). *Performative listening: Hearing others in qualitative research*. New York: Peter Lang.

McRae, C., & Nainby, K. (2015). Engagement beyond interruption: A performative perspective on listening and ethics. *Educational Studies: A Journal of the American Educational Studies Association, 5*(2), 168–184.

Monson, I. (2007). Hearing, seeing, and perceptual agency. *Critical Inquiry, 34,* S36–S58.

Peters, J. D. (2015). *The marvelous clouds: Toward a philosophy of elemental media.* Chicago: The University of Chicago.

Pineau, E. L. (2002). Critical performative pedagogy: Fleshing out the politics of liberatory education. In N. Stucky & C. Wimmer (Eds.), *Teaching performance studies* (pp. 41–54). Carbondale, IL: Southern Illinois University.

Pineda, R. D. (2009). Will they see me coming? Do they know I'm running? Los Lobos and the performance of m*estizaje* identity through journey. *Text and Performance Quarterly, 29*(2), 183–200.

Shoemaker, D. (2010). Queer punk macha femme: Leslie Mah's musical performance in Tribe 8. *Cultural Studies <=>Critical Methodologies, 10*(4), 295–306.

Small, C. (1998). *Musicking: The meanings of performing and listening.* Middletown, CT: Wesleyan University.

Spry, T. (2010). Call it swing: A jazz blues autoethnography. *Cultural Studies <=>Critical Methodologies, 10*(4), 271–282.

Stinson, S. W. (1995). Body of knowledge. *Educational Theory, 45*(1), 43–54.

Stockfelt, O. (1997). Adequate modes of listening (A. Kassabian & L. G. Svendsen, Trans.). In D. Schwarz, A. Kassabian, & L. Siegel (Eds.), *Keeping score: Music, disciplinarity, culture* (pp. 129–146). Charlottesville, VA: University of Virginia.

Sudnow, D. (1993). *The ways of the hand: The organization of improvised conduct.* Cambridge: The MIT.

Walser, R. (1991). The body in the music: Epistemology and musical semiotics. *College Music Symposium, 31,* 117–126.

Warren, J. T. (1999). The body politic: Performance, pedagogy, and the power of enfleshment. *Text and Performance Quarterly, 19,* 257–266.

Warren, J. T. (2003). *Performing purity: Whiteness, pedagogy, and the reconstitution of power.* New York: Peter Lang.

Willis, P. (1981). *Learning to labor: How working class kids get working class jobs.* New York: Columbia University.

CHAPTER 5

Crafting Pictures and Reflexivity

This chapter focuses on the pedagogical function of creative practices and performances of crafting. The practice space for crafting and handmade art offers a metaphor for thinking through the ways artful and creative practices enable new ways of reflexively and critically thinking about, understanding, and making sense of the world and our interactions with others. In particular, we discuss the practice of card-making and our collaborative process of developing a stop-motion animation video. The process of creating handmade cards and stop-motion animation offers insights regarding the development of creative and critical pedagogies. In this chapter, we describe the challenges and questions that emerge during our crafting practices as examples of the kinds of questions and reflexive process that become possible in the practice space of sustained crafting and handmade art practices. We end this chapter with an invitation for engagement. We argue for the development of future practice sessions of crafting as a generative approach to refining and critically thinking about classroom practices, pedagogical interaction, and processes of learning.

Agenda

1. Warm-up
2. Crafting as critical pedagogy
3. Cultivating craft, cultivating repetition
4. Stop-motion: Playing with craft and critical pedagogy
5. Engagement: Creating a crafting workshop
6. Closing

© The Author(s) 2017   97
C. McRae and A. Huber, *Creating Performances for Teaching and Learning,*
Creativity, Education and the Arts, DOI 10.1007/978-3-319-54561-5_5

WARM-UP

Turning to Touch

This practice session begins with a tactile warm-up. How do we encounter touch? How do we touch others and objects? What materials do we touch each day? What textures do we engage by choice? What textures do we engage by necessity? How do these repeated tactile experiences influence how we understand the world? How do we perceive touch when beginning a new practice? How are we aware of touch when the practice is established? Often, once a craft or a crafting practice becomes routine, we no longer attend to specific ways we must negotiate touch and tactile movement to get to anticipated results. Through the repetition of specific practices, our consciousness of touch diminishes and becomes normalized. However, when developing a craft, tactile senses are necessarily heightened, as we become viscerally aware of the ways our body must move. As a pedagogical move, this warm-up is offered as a place to begin interrogating the role of touch in our everyday practices.

Clench your fists.

Take a deep breath.

Release your fingers.

Exhale.

What are you touching at present?

What are the first things you notice? The pads of your fingers on the page or the computer screen? The texture of the book you're reading as you flip through the pages? Are you sitting at a desk or a table? Do you notice the texture of this structure? Do you notice the way your legs and arms are positioned on your chair? Perhaps one of your appendages has fallen asleep? What are your feet touching? The inside of your shoes? The carpet, tile, laminate, or wood floor? Can you feel the texture of your lips as your press them together while working? Does your mouth touch the side of a glass or mug as you sip your favorite beverage? Do you feel the weight of your clothing hanging off your body? Or stray hair brushing your neck? Do you feel warm sweat trickling down your spine or goose bumps rising off your skin? What things are you touching? What objects do you touch on a day-to-day basis?

Clench your fists.

Take a deep breath.

Release your fingers.

Exhale.

When is touch significant?

What kinds of touch have been significant to you? What types of touch do you find memorable? How has touch informed your experiences? What memories of touch linger or haunt? A first kiss? A burn during a cooking experience? A lesson in painting, weaving, or sculpting? Maybe you remember the feeling of your favorite childhood blanket or plaything, its fuzzy or worn fabric as you moved it through your fingers and against your face for comfort? Or, perhaps you remember the touch of a particular family member? Callused, gnarled fingers that once clutched, shook, or patted your own hand? Velvety-soft, paper-thin, wrinkled cheeks that once brushed your lips upon hellos, goodbyes, and long stays?

Clench your fists.

Take a deep breath.

Release your fingers.

Exhale.

When does touch disappear?

What do you touch from day-to-day that you no longer notice? Consider everyday practices, like holding a toothbrush, or silverware, or a pencil. How do these things feel? Do you remember learning to use these everyday objects? When their touch was new? Try to think back on early touch. Try to think about how repetitions of touch become normalized.

For instance, think back on first time you held a pencil. Did you hold it with a tight grip? Or did you hold the pencil with a wobbly and uncertain grip as you tried to make it function in the way it was intended? Do you remember holding a ridged pencil or a smooth one? Did you try to hold in your fist or between thumb and index fingers? How many repetitions did it take before the pencil no longer felt like a foreign object thrust between your fingers? A few hours? A week? A month?

Pick up a pencil now. How do you do you hold it? What does it feel like? What is the grain like? What is the texture like? What do you notice about the way you hold this pencil? How has your experience holding this specific object changed over time? Did a particular instance change the way you touch and hold this object? When? Why? Perhaps you broke a finger or sprained a wrist. Perhaps you had to, at some point, re-learn to hold a pencil. Or, perhaps, you rarely use a pencil anymore. When and why does our awareness of touch emerge, fade, and re-emerge?

Clench your fists.

Take a deep breath.

Release your fingers.

Exhale.

Debriefing the Warm-up

Touch pervades our everyday experience. We can locate touch in the immediate present, and in the ways that touch frames our memories from the past. The prompts in this warm-up are designed to draw attention to the role touch plays in our daily practices and established routines. We offer these prompts as a place to focus on our tactile practices as a place to begin thinking about the relevance of touch, and about how we might engage in touch as a pedagogical act and generative endeavor.

This warm-up sets the groundwork for our discussion of crafting in three ways. First, this warm-up draws our attention to the impact of embodiment and touch within our everyday experience. Second, focusing on new tactile practices highlights the importance of repetition (and rehearsal) in developing a craft. Third, focusing on established practices requires reflection on and contemplation of the meaningfulness of repeated touch.

Warming-up as Repetition

In any pedagogical practice, warm-up exercises cultivate routine through repetition. Warm-ups are often repeated over time and incorporated each session, similar to the organization of this book. Warm-ups, like the one above, also frequently include repetition in them. The use of repetition in a warm-up exercise serves several functions: to focus attention, to reset expectations, and to transform perspectives.

By repeating gesture, words, images, or actions, participants are able to focus their attention in specific ways. For instance, in the warm-up above, the repetition of the stanza: "clench your fists/take a deep breath/release your fingers/exhale," asks participants to pay attention to their bodies in terms of embodied tension and breathing.

Repetition also functions to reset expectations and prepare participants for what is to come. In other words, repetition sets up a transition between one idea or exercise and the next. In the warm-up above, repetition of the stanza helps to transition between three different tactile exercises. The repetition readies the participant to reset and refocus for the next prompt.

Finally, repetition is transformative. Repetition works in service of developing ideas and transforming perspectives. In repeating something over and over, not only is the specific something re-made, but something new is also made. For example, when knitting, not only are the knit and purl stitches made each time, their repetitions form an altogether new piece, such as a scarf or blanket. Similarly, repetitions in warm-ups transform what was known into something new. In the warm-up above, for instance, participants' may develop a changed sense of embodiment and awareness.

Each creative practice necessitates the development of any variety of crafts. All crafting requires rehearsal and repetition of action(s) to try to perfect an art or technique. Slowing down and repeating a particular action (or series of actions) compels us not only to reflect on which strategies work and which do not, but to focus our attention, reset expectations, and transform our perspectives. Through these repetitions, we may begin to engage reflexively with our own subjectivities, ideologies, and social positions. This reflexive engagement opens up the possibility of critical pedagogy that works toward the enactment of social justice.

CRAFTING AS CRITICAL PEDAGOGY

Craft and crafting may be broadly defined acts and activities. For the purposes of our project, we define and understand craft as practices that include handmade arts that may include but are not limited to fiber arts (knitting, crochet, embroidery, sewing, etc.), paper crafts (card-making, origami, *papier mâché*, etc.), and other homemade, or even amateur, artistic projects including digital forms of artmaking (animation, collage, etc.). The characteristic of these practices that is of particular interest to our project is the embodied and *performed* aspects of craft. Like Pelias & Shaffer's (2007) discussion of the expanded role and definition of text in genres of performance emerging from performance art, our understanding of craft as performance centers on the role of the body as text (pp. 166–167). By defining and focusing on craft as a performance, our goal is to understand the pedagogical implications and possibilities of the creative processes of crafting. As Pelias and Shaffer (2007) explain regarding body art, "By placing taken-for-granted behaviors in an aesthetic context, both performers and audiences are able to reconsider their nature" (p. 167). We extend this further to consider the nature of craft as a pedagogical process and practice and how crafting can function as a critical pedagogy.

Craft is related, as Peters (2015) notes, to notions of technique, artistry, and mastery (p. 87). Developing a craft leads to productive accomplishment. In terms of performance, craft over time may be practiced and refined in order to yield particular desired results and outcomes. For example, I may learn the craft of knitting and through practice and repetition, and I may refine this craft so that I may produce desired outcomes like a scarf or a hat. In this way, the performance of crafting may be understood in terms of techniques, processes, and the accomplishment of particular tasks.

Craft and crafting also present the opportunity for conceptual and theoretical work. In his discussion of vernacular theory, McLaughlin (1996) explains: "Culture creates subjects who can in certain situations discern the power of culture itself" (p. 164). In other words, the opportunity for theorizing the effects and implications of culture exists for members and participants of a range of cultural formations. He goes on to specify, "Vernacular theorists are too enmeshed in the culture to be 'free' of it, but that is precisely the ground of their theoretical project. They are insiders, asking questions in local circumstances, challenging the local rules" (p. 165). McLaughlin's discussion of vernacular theory and theorists is offered as an opening for expanding notions of theory, as more than an exclusively academic endeavor. In addition to engaging in particular techniques and creative processes, the crafting performer can also engage in vernacular modes of theory. Being enmeshed in a particular craft enables the crafting performer to generate theory from and about that craft. For example, knitters are well positioned, as experts, to generate theories about their performances of knitting. Vernacular theories of crafting may include acts of questioning the cultural values, politics, and implications of crafting practices. For example, crafting performers might interrogate notions of identity (how and why are certain crafts gendered, racialized, sexualized?), privilege (who has the financial means to craft?), and power (what values are reproduced, included, and excluded in and by crafting?) that surround cultural forms of crafting.

Another way the crafting performer can engage in the work of theorizing is through the use of craft as a method for analyzing and critiquing culture. Crafting may be used in order to directly address cultural concerns, values, and issues. For example, in her edited collection *Craftivism: The Art of Craft and Activism,* Greer (2014) presents essays and example of the ways crafting can be employed "for the greater good" (p. 7). Practices such as textile graffiti, including yarn bombing, in which handmade pieces are purposefully juxtaposed in public spaces offer critique and commentary on cultural institutions and politics (Woodhouse 2016). In addition to using craft as an explicit form of activism, crafting may also be employed as a way of creating new understandings and ways of knowing through the use of repetition, jux-taposition, and failure.

In his discussion of the rhetoric of craft emerging from the Arts & Crafts movement of the nineteenth century, Rice (2015) resolves, "Arts & Crafts fostered the ever-present critique of consumption by situat-ing the industrial as always antithetical to the artisanal. The industrial is impure; the artisanal is pure" (p. 219). Craft, and the rhetoric sur-rounding crafts and crafting are in part linked to a moralizing critique of consumerism, and the practice of privileging crafted goods. For exam-ple, Rice points specifically to the rhetorical function of craft regarding the production and consumption of food and beverages. He then points to the contradictions that craft food and beverage production present, namely that these are always also a form of industry. Rice troubles the notion of craft rhetoric as critique saying:

> Craft rhetoric—with its contradictory positions—is not necessarily a critical gesture. Craft rhetoric is a series of contradictions. And while critique may be the preferred tool for cultural examination, contradiction might offer better insight into how food and beverage cultures function rhetorically. (p. 221)

Though Rice is specifically interested in the rhetoric of craft in the con-text of food and beverage, his insights regarding the function of this rhetoric is relevant for consideration and application of craft as a kind of performance. If the rhetorical function of craft is contradiction not critique, then engaging in craft presents possibilities for enacting perfor-mance and critical pedagogy in ways that feature contradiction, disrup-tion, and interrogation. In other words, crafts and crafting are creative acts that work in the service of critical pedagogy not only as modes of analysis and evaluation. These acts also draw our attention to, reproduce, and disrupt cultural values, practices, and ideologies.

Kilgard (2009) engages the craft of collage as a heuristic and generative paradigm for performance studies research. Though collage is a particular form of artmaking and performance work, the aspects of collage that Kilgard finds useful for theorizing the work of performance are similarly useful for theorizing performances of crafting as critical pedagogy. She explains:

> I posit four facets of collage as paradigmatic for performance studies: 1) Collage involves examining the (at least) double life of constitutive com-ponents; 2) Collage is a sensual/sensory/embodied practice; 3) Collage

involves juxtapositions and relationships of elements in time and space; 4) Collage is unsettled. These elements of collage are not mutually exclusive. Nor are they exhaustive. (p. 11)

These four features demonstrate the ways collage functions as a method of performance research, and though these elements emerge specifically from the practice of collage they are still relevant for theorizing crafting as similarly a method of performance research and pedagogy. In other words, collage may deal explicitly in these characteristics, but these characteristics can also explain *how* crafting works as a performance method.

First Kilgard (2009) argues, "Collage involves examining the (at least) double life of constitutive components" (p. 11). In the context of collage, multiple elements work individually and together to constitute a variety of possible meanings and interpretations (p. 3). In terms of a broad definition of crafting as a method of performance research and critical pedagogy, this element of collage points to the constitutive nature of crafting practices. In other words, crafting always presents the possibility for creating a multiplicity of meanings. For example, crafting may be a question of constituting a particular artifact, but the context of the production, and the use of particular materials also work to create various meanings. As a method of research and critical pedagogy, crafting is a practice that is invested, like collage, in the examination and consideration of the implications made possible by the performance of crafting. This practice asks: What can be learned by engaging in this activity? How is this activity shaped by the context of practice? How does this activity work to re-define spaces and interactions?

The second element Kilgard (2009) reveals regarding collage as heuristic and paradigm for performance studies is the idea that, "Collage is a sensual/sensory/embodied practice" (p. 11). The acts of making collage and of crafting are both physical performances (p. 13). Each different craft-making practice asks the performer to engage in different kinds of tasks. For example, collage involves searching, cutting, tearing, arranging, and fixing (p. 13). Knitting requires the tactile interaction with yarn and needles. Card-making includes the folding and manipulation of paper and other materials. Even crafting in a digital context entails a tactile interaction with keyboards, mices, and touch screens. The embodied and sensual nature of crafting is notable as a part of a learning and research process that centers on inquiry via experience. As a sensual and embodied practice, crafting raises the following kinds of questions for the researcher/student: What physical actions and interactions does this practice require? What parts of the body does crafting draw attention to? How does the body struggle in crafting? How does the body succeed? What might these physical tasks reveal about the process of learning? What does the tactile reveal about research?

The third element Kilgard (2009) presents as a feature of collage in terms of performance is that "Collage involves juxtapositions and relationships of elements in time and space" (p. 11). Kilgard goes on to demonstrate, "As a compositional strategy of collaging, juxtaposition involves deliberately putting disparate things/texts next to each other without direct connective material with the belief that they will resonate with each other in some way" (p. 15). The compositional use of juxtaposition in collage for generative purposes is relevant to an understanding of crafting as performance, not because all crafting practices use juxtaposition, but because the performance of crafting presents the opportunity for juxtaposition with questions of research and teaching. In other words, juxtaposing a performance of crafting with a specific research question may engender a variety of resonating themes and discoveries. As Kilgard says of juxtaposition in collage, juxtaposition of crafting practices can be pedagogical (p. 15). Juxtaposing crafting with research may raise the following questions: What might a crafting practice teach or suggest about a seemingly unrelated research topic? How might a crafting practice function as a method of research? What does crafting make possible in addressing a particular research question? What happens when a crafting practice is juxtaposed with an abstract theory or claim?

The final element presented by Kilgard for considering collage as a paradigm for performance studies research is the notion that "Collage is unsettled" (p. 11). She argues collage is a form that is constantly open to question:

> Collage also has the power to put everything into question by removing texts from one (perhaps familiar) context and putting them in another. This calls on the audience to participate in the act of questioning, asking them to examine their own associations and experiences with the constitutive elements of the collage as well as the themes, ideas, and texts themselves presented in the collage work. (p. 4)

Collage creates an opportunity for the audience to question or explore the implications of the text, and for the audience to question or explore the implications of their responses. Collage is, in Barthes's (1974) terms a writerly text (p. 5). In other words, this is a text that presents the opportunity for the audience to write their own meanings as they encounter the text. Not all crafting performances yield unsettled texts; however, this element of collage points to the research and pedagogical implications of employing crafting performances to address and engage research questions. Juxtaposing crafting with research presents the opportunity for productively unsettling the process of research and learning. Using crafting to engage in research is a tactic for calling the researcher to question the way they approach the research process, and to question the research (Kilgard 2009, p. 4).

Engaging in crafting as a research process is not unlike the artistic practice of ekphrasis in which one art form is used to represent another form of art. Using music to represent painting, or using poetry to represent sculpture are both forms of ekphrasis. Holman Jones (2005) considers the implications of engaging ekphrastic texts in performance, and asks:

> And what happens when we perform an ekphrastic text? What happens when we perform the artist performing the artist, repeating the act of connection and creation, breaking that experience out of one form and context and remaking it in another? Perhaps we create a critical ekphrasis, a performance that moves through *mimesis* (imitation) and *poiesis* (creation) to *kinesis* (movement). (Conquergood 1992, p. 84; Holman Jones 2005, p. 214)

The function of a critical ekphrasis is to generate new possibilities by shifting artistic modes and contexts, and by exploring and expanding points of contact and creation. Performances of crafting similarly present the opportunity for a critical performance and pedagogy that works toward movement in research. Crafting, understood and engaged as a performance of research, presents a critical pedagogy that takes seriously the potential for learning about process, embodiment, juxtaposition, and unsettling of the taken-for-granted and unexamined assumptions of research and learning.

In the following sections, we discuss two examples of our use of crafting in research: card-making and stop-motion animation. In these sections, we focus on two aspects of crafting that are particularly generative as features of a critical pedagogy: repetition and reflexivity.

CULTIVATING CRAFT, CULTIVATING REPETITION

In my family, we send greeting cards. Over the years, I have sent and received hundreds, if not thousands of greeting cards. From the time I was little, I remember receiving an assortment of cards for all occasions from a variety of relations. My paternal grandmother's cards were always flowery, with equally ornate illustrations, and often were accompanied by a longer letter either to me or to my parents about the comings and goings of the extended family and people from my dad's youth. My maternal grandparents sent cards with funny homemade illustrations, which read more like pictogram puzzles for us to decipher. My aunts each sent their own preferred style of card, which ranged from the religious message to the dirty joke. Before she died, when I was ten, my godmother was the queen of cards, taking time to postcards for most federal holidays including the obscure or unusual ones we did not recognize until her card arrived. She sent playful "kid cards," with bright colors and silly sayings. She also always included gum or stickers, which made her cards exciting to receive even before I could read. Moving away from home I started to receive cards from my parents and younger sister, mostly for birthdays, but sometimes just because.

It has always been a thrill to check the mailbox and find something special just for me. When sending cards, I like to imagine a similar pleasure rising in the faces of my friends and family as they file through bills, ads, and junk mail to find they have received something more personal. I started making my own cards when I moved out of state. I wanted to connect with family back in Iowa, especially my grandparents, none of whom owned a computer or a cell phone. At first, I spent exorbitant amounts of time in the card aisles of the local grocery and drugstores trying to find cards which relayed the perfect message, even though the card was often the vehicle for a longer letter inquiring about my family and friends, and offering some details of my new life. For a while, I was sending one or two cards a week, but finding just the right card was becoming more difficult and more expensive. Out of a desire to personalize my messages, I headed to the local craft store.

My foray into card-making started small with a couple large packages of pre-folded blank cards with envelopes, a few rubber stamps, and black ink. Now my collection has grown to occupy several plastic storage containers, and a large cabinet full of fountain pens and refills, cardstock, paper, blank cards and envelopes, inks in a variety of colors, and a growing assortment of rubber stamps. Friends and family often give me stamps to add to my collection. And, I can often be found checking out bargain bins, sales, and online specialty shops for special card-making projects. I have a stash of handmade thank you notes and birthday cards to send out at a moment's notice.

Though I enjoy making cards, it takes time. It takes time to make each card. It takes time to learn the feel for the materials with which I am working. It takes time to learn the limits of my body. And it takes more time still to find ways to change those limits and create a routine for crafting. I was not born making cards. I fashion myself into a card maker through repetition. Even with careful repetition and practice this tactile craft is not does not yield perfect results. My handmade cards are never quite as precise as a machine-manufactured card. There's often an ink blotch here, or a slanted line there. I think this is part of the beauty in the craft, being privy to the flaw. For the flaw reveals the process. Flaws draw attention to repetition, which as McRae (2010) argues, highlights process: how particular processes come to be, and how they may be changed (pp. 179–180). Each flaw in a repetition reveals the possibility for change. For me a flaw offers something changed, something new. In what follows, I describe my own process for making cards, as a way to illustrate the ways in which we may begin attending to process, repetition, and flaw.

Even though I make cards for dozens of occasions, each project follows a similar pattern:

Step One: Generate Ideas and Gather Materials

Generate initial ideas for the card's theme.

Sketch ideas.

Perform an Internet search of the card genre (i.e., party invitations, holiday greetings, and announcements)

Jot a list of favorable ideas.

Gauge the time frame.

Jot a list of doable ideas.

Make a list of materials.

Revise initial sketches.

Gather materials.

Brainstorm the front matter.

List possibilities for the inscription.
Add to the list of materials.
Purchase supplemental craft material.
Order appropriate rubber stamps.
Buy two or three small reams of cardstock.
Acquire or create complementary envelopes.

Step Two: Experiment With Ideas and Make Initial Choices

Set up a workspace.
Spread out all available materials.
Sketch a working idea for the whole card (complete with message and illustration/design).
Measure envelopes.
Sketch a prototype for a card that will fit inside your envelope.
Carefully measure cardstock.
Mark dimensions with a pencil.
Make a template for the card.
Cut out a number of cards.
Create a series of rough prototypes. (Don't bother to measure anything; this prototype is to see how your working idea looks on the card.)
Decide on a prototype.
Make choices as to font, placement, design, etc.

Step Three: Replicate the Prototype; Make the Cards

Use the card template to make as many cards as you will need.
Make extras; some cards will be scrapped.
Measure carefully.
Cut each card by hand.
Verify that each card fits inside the envelope.
Stack all usable cards.
Take a break if necessary; this process takes a considerable amount of time.
Center your title matter.
Use a small ruler to carefully measure the distance across.
On each card measure the center point.
Print title matter, cut out, and paste on the top of the cards. Center the printed title matter by measuring the length of the message in

comparison with the length of the card. Adjust it to be in the middle of the card. Or,

Use a card stencil that doubles a ruler, center the stencil in the middle of the card, and then hand write title matter on each. (If writing by hand, it is necessary to also practice with the card stencil ahead of time to establish the font should look.)

Make extras; some cards will be scrapped.

After all cards have been titled, go back through and see whether there are any major outliers.

Toss outliers.

Stack all usable cards.

Take a break if necessary; this process takes a considerable amount of time.

Print additional messages, cut out, and paste on the cards.

Or,

Use a do-it-yourself stamp kit; create stamps with the other messages that will populate the card.

Select a round, square, rectangular, or oval stamp holder.

Using tweezers, insert individual letters to create the message.

Adjust the spacing of the letters.

Test the stamp on scrap paper.

Re-adjust the letters for spacing and coherence.

Stamp the cards with titles.

For each card, press firmly down on the ink to get an adequate amount on the letters.

Press the inked stamps firmly and evenly on each card.

Make extras; some cards will be scrapped.

After stamping all the cards, go back through and look for major outliers.

Toss outliers.

Stack all usable cards.

Take a break if necessary; this process takes a considerable amount of time.

Print illustrations, cut out and paste on cards.

Or,

Use a ruler to center a stamp design.

If repeating a stamp, measure and lightly mark an equal length between each stamp to try to keep the design consistent.

Select ink(s) for each stamp.

Test the stamp on scrap paper.

For each stamp, press firmly down on the ink.

Press the inked stamps firmly and evenly on each card.

Repeat until the correct number of stamps is achieved.

Make extras; some cards will be scrapped.

After stamping all the cards, go back through and look for major outliers.

Toss outliers.

Stack all usable cards.

Take a break if necessary; this process takes a considerable amount of time.

Step Four: Address and Send Cards

Stack all envelopes.

Print return address labels and attach to each envelope. Or,

Use a personalized return address stamp.

Select ink.

Test the stamp on scrap paper.

For each stamp, press firmly down on the ink.

Press the inked stamps firmly and evenly on each card.

Make extras; some envelopes will be scrapped.

Stack all usable envelopes.

Take a break if necessary; this process takes a considerable amount of time.

Print address labels and attach to each envelope. Or,

Center the card stencil on the envelope.

Measure the distance from each side to find the center.

Use the card stencil to handwrite each address on each envelope.

Rewrite envelopes on which mistakes are made.

Stack all usable envelopes.

Attach postage to each envelope.

Post the cards.

Begin the next project.

Though crafting cards started out as a way to add a personal touch to the everyday greeting card, I realize that this practice can also function as an analogy for my approach to critical pedagogy. Card-making is a heuristic process, which involves a significant amount of experimentation, repetition, and revising. Like a commitment to critical pedagogy, it is an ongoing project that takes up space not only in my mind but in our home. It takes up physical and emotional space. A hodgepodge of materials is always strewn out all over the house, and often nothing is ever quite tidied up or put back until new organizational patterns or configurations take shape. As with critical pedagogy card-making takes time; it is generative and calculated. I often have a clear idea of why I am creating a particular card, but I am not always sure how to go about doing it, or what the end result will look like. In experimenting with ideas and materials, themes start to emerge and patterns begin to form. I can begin to measure margins, stamp with accuracy, and repeat ideas. And, yet my repetitions are not perfect. Nor do I want them to be. They are imperfections that then take on new or alternative meanings. I appreciate the process of revising, repeating, changing things, and starting again. This is what critical pedagogy asks me to do, to revise, repeat, change, and start again.

STOP-MOTION: PLAYING WITH CRAFT AND CRITICAL PEDAGOGY

Tripod (click) …
unfold (click) …
set down (click) …
camera bag (click) …
unzip (click) …
remove camera (click) …
remove lens cover (click) …
attach to tripod (click) …
adjust lights (click) …
position opening image (click) …

Stop-motion animation is a form of animation that features the process of manipulating physical objects and taking a series of photographs in order to create frames that can be replayed at a high speed in order to animate the images. This technique is used to animate films using a variety of materials including, but not limited to, clay, puppets, and people. Throughout this section, we work with the halting esthetic of stop-motion animation in our writing. This writing works to consider and convey the formal effect and implications of the incremental and transformative possibilities of the repetitive, sequential, and deliberately manipulated images in terms of pedagogical interaction and practice.

Popular examples of stop-motion animation include (click) …
the 1964 television Christmas special (click) …

Rudolph the Red-Nosed Reindeer (click) ...
feature films such as (click) ...
Tim Burton's *The Nightmare Before Christmas* (1993) (click) ...
The Box Trolls (2014) (click) ...
Kubo and the Two Strings (2016) (click)
short films including (click) ...
Fresh Guacamole (2013) by PES (click) ...

Troubling Stop-Motion Animation

Stop-motion animation is also a technique used in a variety of educational contexts as a form of experiential and engaged learning. For example,
Kamp and Deaton (2013) (click) ...
present an activity (click) ...
in which biology students (click) ...
create stop-motion animation (click) ...
of mitosis (click) ...
the process of cellular division (click) ...
Ivashkevich (2015) (click) ...
describes a process (click) ...
in which preservice art educators (click) ...
use stop-motion animation (click) ...
to investigate popular toys (click) ...
as sites of cultural production (click) ...
and possible sites (click) ...
of cultural resistance (click) ...
Blair (2014) (click) ...
details the use of stop-motion animation (click) ...
in conjunction with autoethnography (click) ...
as a method of reflexive inquiry (click) ...
for preservice art educators (p. 8) (click) ...
The deliberate process and segmented form of creating stop-motion animation lend itself to a wide range of classroom assignments and research questions. Stop-motion animation offers a process that can be operationalized, repeated, and used to present discrete findings to research questions.
With stop-motion as an educational (click) ...
experimental form (click) ...

students can be asked to (click) …
collaborate (click) …
create storyboards (click) …
(Kamp and Deaton 2013; Ivashkevich 2015) (click) …
engage digital technologies (click) …
(Kamp and Deaton 2013; Ivashkevich 2015; Brownlee 2016) (click) …
edit (click) …
produce (click) …
present findings (click) …
offer feedback (click) …
revise (click) …

Stop-motion animation is a form of performance that is characterized by touch, movement, and repetition. Pedagogically, this form of performance may be used in order to replicate knowledge and understanding of particular concepts. Stop-motion animation can be used to create models, to represent findings, or to sequentially narrate interpretations. This application of a performance technique in pedagogy is an effective strategy for engaging concepts in ways that are embodied, specific, and applied. However, the use of performance, including stop-motion animation, in pedagogical contexts can also generate new and unexpected forms of knowledge and ways of thinking.

Kilgard (2011) calls for a troubling of performance pedagogy through the use of chaos as a way of enacting and acknowledging the theoretical complexity of teaching in ways that are embodied and performative (p. 220). In her departure from traditional approaches to performance pedagogies that emphasize embodiment as a way of learning and knowing, Kilgard argues for the epistemological value of chaos that emerges in performance pedagogies stating, "an orientation to chaos opens us to the fractal and rhizomatic knowledges that are (re)iterated through embodied engagement and not only through linear and hierarchical arguments" (p. 220). In other words, chaos is a way of knowing and learning that values embodiment, multiple points of understanding, and the possibility for pedagogical interactions that are generative rather than predictive. This troubling of performance pedagogy in terms of chaos helps frame for us the ways stop-motion animation might also work as a creative critical pedagogy that moves beyond linear representations of understanding.

Answering a research question (click) …
Through the use (click) …

Of stop-motion animation (click) …
May present a linear answer (click) …
A coherent story (click) …
and a polished esthetic text (click) …
Stop-motion animation may also (click) …
trouble (click) …
this logical production of findings (click) …
by emphasizing the process (click) …
of touch (click) …
of movement (click) …
and repetition (click) …
as pedagogically (click) …
and theoretically (click) …
meaningful (click) …

One way to trouble stop-motion animation as a representational form of presenting research findings, modeling concepts, and the narration of events is to employ stop-motion animation as a method for answering research questions before findings or results are determined. In other words, stop-motion animation can be used as a process for engaging and exploring research questions. Troubling stop-motion animation asks: what if stop-motion animation is used not for displaying findings, but for displaying the process of finding? What if stop-motion can be used not to model concepts, but to model conceptualizing? Instead of using stop-motion animation to narrate events, what if stop-motion animation is reflexively engaged as the event?

Research and Production

In the fall of 2014, we submit a performance proposal to the Southern States Communication Association conference. The conference theme, "Communication as Art and Craft," presents us with the opportunity to frame our research interests in performance studies and critical pedagogy in terms of craft. We decide to develop a stop-motion animation that uses crafting supplies to explore our ongoing interest in theorizing our critical performance pedagogies. We title the performance: "Glue Sticks, Glitter, and Safety Scissors: Crafting Performance Pedagogy." Our research questions include: When do we craft performance pedagogy? Where do we craft performance pedagogy? How do we theorize performance pedagogy? These are research questions we consider frequently as scholars with interests in performance studies and pedagogy, but this is our first attempt creating stop-motion animation. We decide to test the limits of this performance form as a method of engaging these questions, and so we clear a space on our dining room table.

Aubrey sets a bag (click) ...
full of craft supplies (click) ...
on the table (click) ...
The supplies emerge from the bag (click) ...
glue sticks (click) ...
a jar of silver glitter (click) ...
a pair of safety scissors (click) ...
construction paper (click) ...
a tape dispenser (click) ...
crepe paper (click) ...
a stack of wooden craft sticks (click) ...
a box of crayons (click) ...
a roll of paper (click) ...
a box of markers (click) ...
a skein of yarn (click) ...
knitting needles (click) ...
a jar of rubber cement (click) ...
a bag of pipe cleaners (click) ...

The supplies move (and are moved) into a swirling circle and eventually move off the table except for the wooden craft sticks. In a series of over two thousand pictures, we use each of the craft supplies to create various images and scenes. We create paper dolls out of the construction paper, a scarf with the yarn, and a structure made of craft sticks. The glue stick, the jar of glitter, and the scissors are cast as lead characters throughout the animation. These objects are positioned in order to suggest or signify the ways they might manipulate and interact with the other craft supplies. For example, in one scene the glue stick, jar of glitter, and scissors each move up and across scaffolding created out of the wooden craft sticks.

In order to animate these scenes, we place our camera on a tripod and focus the lens on a set portion of the table approximately two feet by two feet. We adjust the objects on the table, move out of the frame, and take a picture. We then make adjustments to the objects, move out of the frame, and take a picture. For each second of animation, we take approximately thirty-two pictures. Between each picture, we gradually move the objects a centimeter or two here and there, taking into consideration the direction of the movement to be animated. We also make decisions about ways to introduce new objects, how to remove objects, and how the scene will take shape as a somewhat coherent set of movements.

Throughout the production of the animation, we continue to return to our research question: How do we craft our performance pedagogy? We consider ways we might represent our experience of crafting our pedagogy (the sequence of swirling craft supplies suggests the field of possibilities for creating a performance pedagogy). We try to account for our goals (scaffolding as a pedagogical strategy for offering students structures to support their own processes of discovery). We consider the importance of embodiment in our classroom practices (our creation of paper dolls works to suggest the work that goes into creating opportunities in teaching that center on and privilege embodied modes of learning). We attempt to link each series of movements with some theme or goal of our own teaching practices.

Stop-motion animation, as a method, initially leads us to develop answers to our research question in ways that are symbolic and suggestive. Without the use of language, we find it challenging to fully characterize the work and thought that we put into crafting our pedagogy. After putting the photographs into a sequence, we add a soundtrack of instrumental music that we download from an archive of open-access compositions and create a 6-min video for presentation at the conference. The final product has recognizable features of stop-motion animation. The objects are animated, the movements are coherent, and there is a choppy quality to the overall production. What is not overly apparent or clear in this final product is the answer to the question: how do we craft performance pedagogy? However, the process of creating this animated video reveals important insights for us about the work of crafting pedagogy.

Research and Repetition

Aubrey sets a bag (click) …
  After some deliberation (click) …
  Full of craft supplies (click) …
  From our own personal collection (click) …
  On the table (click) …
  A space that we dedicate to the creation of this performance (click) …

The supplies emerge from the bag (click) ...
For the next four months (click) ...
Glue sticks (click) ...
With the help of Chris's brother and sister-in-law (click) ...
A jar of silver glitter (click) ...
Bodies moving out of the frame (click) ...
A pair of safety scissors (click) ...
Bodies moving back into the frame (click) ...
Construction paper (click) ...
Bodies carefully pushing the button on the camera (click) ...
A tape dispenser (click) ...
Viewing the first pictures to check lighting and angles (click) ...
Crepe paper (click) ...
Bodies trying not to run into the tripod (click) ...
A stack of wooden craft sticks (click) ...
Adjusting the camera when it is inevitably bumped (click) ...
A box of crayons (click) ...
A choreography of movement (click) ...
A roll of paper (click) ...
A discussion about what is next (click) ...
A box of markers (click) ...
Where will these objects move (click) ...
A skein of yarn (click) ...
Whose turn is it to take the pictures? (click) ...
Knitting needles (click) ...
Looking through the first fifty pictures (click) ...
A jar of rubber cement (click) ...
What would be a good stopping place for the night? (click) ...
A bag of pipe cleaners (click) ...
Charging the camera battery (click) ...
While the final product did not directly answer the question of how
performance pedagogy is crafted, the process of creating this stop-
motion animation began to reveal, through repetition, important
insights about the production of pedagogy. Crafting a stop-motion animation presented an analogy for the work and time needed for crafting
performance pedagogy. Like creating stop-motion animation, creating
performance pedagogy is a performance of duration. It takes time to
create performance pedagogy, and this pedagogy also develops over
a long period of time. Like creating stop-motion animation, creating

performance pedagogy demands the use of space. Developing pedagogy always requires the use of space, and often this exceeds the institutional boundaries of classrooms and offices. Like creating stop-motion animation, creating performance pedagogy is always dependent on bodies. Performance pedagogy features embodied modes of learning, but it is also important to acknowledge the ways creating this pedagogy offers an embodied mode of learning for us as teachers. Like the creation of stop-motion animation, the creation of performance pedagogy often conceals the labor of production. The constant work of preparing and developing pedagogy is easy to overlook, under-theorize, and ignore; however, this work always matters.

The lessons (click) …
or findings (click) …
made possible by creating stop-motion animation (click) …
emerge in (click) …
and throughout (click) …
the process of making (click) …
the animation (click) …
This method (click) …
engenders conversation (click) …
reflection (click) …
and reflexivity (click) …
about learning (click) …
teaching (click) …
and research (click) …
as creative (click) …
and critical (click) …
acts of crafting (click) …

In this case, our process centered on the question of how we craft performance pedagogy; however, stop-motion animation as a process could offer productive insights about a wide range of research questions. The deliberate movement of objects, the repetition of acts required for capturing pictures, and the consideration of the ways the images might work together are all aspects of this method that present the opportunity for developing and discovering new perspectives and insights.

The critical value of employing a practice like stop-motion animation as a research method lies in the generative possibilities of juxtaposition of the method with research questions and the repetitive characteristics of the process. First, the juxtaposition of stop-motion animation with a range of research questions, including questions that don't seemingly match the method, presents opportunities for discovering points of contact that might otherwise not exist (Kilgard 2009, p. 15) . Realizations that might emerge as metaphors, analogies, or embodied explanations become possible when crafting practices are engaged in order to consider research questions.

Second, the repetitive process of stop-motion animation, like many crafting practices, presents the opportunity for discoveries that materialize in subtle and incremental ways. Each repeated act offers a new opportunity for reflection about process, about research topic, or about method. Each repeated act also presents the possibility for a new perspective about the role of the researcher and the embodied consequences of the act of research. And the duration of the process also allows for connections between research and method to emerge gradually.

Engaging (click) ...
the process (click) ...
of creating (click) ...
stop (click) ...
motion (click) ...
animation (click) ...
as a method of research (click) ...
is a process that (click) ...
privileges (click) ...
findings that are (click) ...
unexpected (click) ...
emergent (click) ...
and multiple (click) ...

ENGAGEMENT: CREATING A CRAFTING WORKSHOP

Engagement Description

The goal of this engagement is to offer a crafting practice session as way to engage with research questions. Crafting provides the opportunity for participants to engage in exploration, experimentation, and research by examining lived experience and everyday objects as indicative of larger cultural phenomena. Crafting workshops can take many forms and incorporate various methods based on the expertise and fluency of the facilitator and participants. For this session, we have designed an engagement around assemblage to introduce facilitators and participants to generating crafting projects. Pelias and Shaffer (2007) discuss the surrealist art form of assemblage as an "everyday life sculpture" in which artists collect everyday objects and put them together in one scene or setting (p. 163).

The objective in this engagement will be to have participants create small assemblage work within the frame of a diorama. Dioramas, like many other craft projects, invite the creator to examine and take seriously everyday objects, as valuable for understanding and theorizing culture. Dioramas range in size, shape, and content can be found in museums, elementary classrooms, and art galleries. They also offer a place to stage scenes with created and found objects. For this engagement, participants will be asked to generate a diorama that engages a particular research question within a small shoebox-sized container.

Before the practice session, begin gathering an array of crafting materials to get participants started on their various dioramas. Each person will need a shoebox. Other crafting materials will likely evolve with each participant's project. Before the workshop, it will be helpful to solicit materials by providing a list of items to workshop participants. In addition to shoeboxes, consider collecting magazines, newspapers, construction paper, wrapping paper, tissue paper, butcher paper, printer paper, crayons, markers, pencils, charcoal, glue/paste, tape glitter, paper clips, scissors, yarn, stencils, canvases, paint, paintbrushes, found objects (old CDs, cassettes, buttons, scrap paper, photographs), and organic matter (sponges, acorns, rocks, twigs, leaves, seeds, dried or fresh flowers or plants, shells, sand, dirt, etc.).

To lead these workshops, decide on how you want to participants to engage with research. You may develop sessions in which individual research questions emerge from a particular workshop theme. For instance, a theme on gender performance will likely produce a wide variety of research questions and crafting projects that interrogate gender. You may also request that participants bring preformed research questions to the session. For example, you may have worked with the same group of participants in workshop series, or over a period of time, and recognize that each person has fairly defined interests and questions. Alternatively, you may decide to introduce participants to research through crafting by having all participants engage in the same question. Engaging in a similar question will still yield a wide variety of insights, especially since each participant's process and development of craft will be different.

Since we want to introduce the reader to this process of research through craft, this engagement follows the final approach. In this engagement, facilitators will encourage participants to create a craft project around a particular research question: "How does contemporary culture articulate education?" As they begin this project, participants should also consider the following questions: How do individuals experience the educational system? What social and political ideologies inform what it means to educate or become educated? How does the educational system privilege particular groups? What are the limitations of the educational system? What does it mean to become educated? How do current systems of education support ideals of what it means to be educated? How do they fall short? What are the implications for educating others?

Facilitating the Workshop

First, direct participants to work in groups to start generating ideas about the broad question: "How does contemporary culture articulate education?" Explain that each group will be working with a specific question from the list above. Once groups have been divided and assigned a specific question, direct participants to engage crafting materials that have been gathered. As a group have them collect materials that respond to and inform their specific question. When they have collected the materials, keeping in mind their specific question, ask participants to silently assemble a scene, perhaps on a table or on the floor. Limit the time groups have to generate these scenes. When the time is up ask participants to discuss their scene together. Label each group's work with the specific question to which the craft project responds so that the group members can keep it mind during their conversation. Consider the following questions to guide discussion:

- How would you describe the scene you see? How would you describe how objects are positioned?
- What themes are suggested bringing these objects together?
- What responses might these objects offer your specific question?
- What answers might this scene as a whole offer your specific question?

Second, after groups have discussed their own scenes, have the groups rotate so that they are able to observe another group's project. Give them several minutes to experience the scene, perhaps jotting down some notes. Encourage the participants to avoid discussing the scene with their other group members. After they have had a little time to experience the new scene, prompt the group to add to the assemblage and make adjustments based on their perspectives. As in the first iteration of this activity, limit the time these groups have to make changes. When the time expires, ask the group to again discuss the scene. Consider having them respond to the same prompting questions as before, and adding one or two new prompts as well:

- What changes did your group make? What objects were added? Was anything subtracted?
- In what ways did the changes shift the themes that the scene suggested?

If there is time, ask the groups to again shift to another scene, and repeat the process until all groups have had the opportunity to experience, add to, and discuss all of the pieces. Then, lead the entire group in a debriefing session, and move on to direct participants to developing their own individual diorama projects.

Using the small group assemblage activity as a model, direct the participants back to consider the broad research question and ask them to craft their own dioramas. First, ask the participants to pull materials from the group assemblage projects and add other materials that are relevant to their own perspectives. In some cases, this will be a challenge since a shoebox diorama does not allow for as much space as the larger assemblage projects. Therefore, encourage participants to build their ideas through simplifications or metonymic suggestions, in which a piece stands in for the whole. Though some objects may be stationary, it is also a good idea to encourage participants to attach their objects to their shoeboxes so they be moved and easily re-assembled. By the end of the workshop, the participants will each have a sculpture to be displayed, shared, and discussed. Direct the participants to create a "gallery" in which all of the dioramas can be displayed and experienced. After observing these individual dioramas prompt participants to further engage their research through the following questions:

- How did you engage with the dioramas? Did you touch, or smell, or listen to, or observe visually?
- In what way(s) did your interaction with the diorama affect your interpretation of the scene?

- Which dioramas stuck out to you? How would you describe these scenes? What trends or themes were being developed?
- What insights did these dioramas offer in terms of "contemporary articulations of education?"
- In what ways did creating these dioramas echo support a particular learning style/experience? (How) does that affect your understanding of education?

CLOSING

A practice session of crafting emphasizes the ways crafting practices, or handmade arts, are accomplished in and through performance as a generative pedagogical endeavor. Crafting offers possibilities for developing educational practices and performances that feature embodiment, touch, and repetition. In particular, crafting presents an embodied method of teaching and learning that is not only a creative way to engage particular content, but crafting also offers a heuristic for discovering new insights about pedagogical practices and research questions. Crafting can serve as a method for creating and refining a performance pedagogy by attending to questions of embodiment, touch, and repetition. The ways bodies learn and perform while crafting can reveal the ways bodies learn and perform in a variety of educational contexts. The sensory focus on touch in crafting can point to the ways touch functions as an often taken-for-granted mode of learning and discovery. The use of repetition in crafting as a technique of production can draw attention to the function of repetition in a variety of contexts.

In addition to developing pedagogical strategies by engaging with crafting, a practice session of crafting also invites the use of crafting as a method of discovery, learning, and research. In this chapter, we focus on our examples of crafting in terms of card-making and stop-motion animation; however, other crafting practices present similarly productive possibilities for rethinking pedagogical practices. The juxtaposition of crafting practices, like card-making and stop-motion animation, with seemingly unrelated research questions can yield critical insights and discoveries. What is critically significant about this kind of juxtaposition is the use of a creative practice in order to engage in educational practices in ways that are not prescriptive or singular. Rather than simply use crafting to represent findings, display answers, or narrate experiences; juxtaposition allows crafting to be employed as a generative process that can yield multiple answers and new questions. A practice session of crafting works against the reduction in crafting to a secondary role in pedagogical contexts and works toward the use of crafting as a critically meaningful mode of learning.

REFERENCES

Barthes, R. (1974). S/Z: An essay. (R. Miller, Trans.) *New York: Farrar, Straus, and Giroux.*

Blair, J. M. (2014). Animated autoethnographies: Stop motion animation as a tool for self-inquiry and personal evolution. *Art Education, 67,* 6–13.

Brownlee, S. (2016). Amateurism and the aesthetics of Lego stop-motion on YouTube. *Film Criticism, 40*(2), 1–21.

Conquergood, D. (1992). Ethnography, rhetoric, and performance. *Quarterly Journal of Speech, 78,* 80–97.

Greer, B. (2014). Knitting craftivism: From my sofa to yours. In B. Greer (Ed.), *Craftivism: The art of craft and activism* (pp. 7–10). Vancouver, BC: Arsenal Pulp Press.

Holman Jones, S. (2005). Autoethnography: Making the personal political. In N. K. Denzin & Y. S. Lincoln (Eds.), *Handbook of qualitative research* (pp. 763–791). Thousand Oaks, CA: Sage.

Ivashkevich, O. (2015). Engaging a prosumer: Preservice art teachers interrogate popular toys through stop-motion animation. *Art Education, 68*(2), 42–47.

Kamp, B. L., & Deaton, C. M. (2013). Move, stop, learn: Illustrating mitosis through stop-motion animation. *Science Activities, 50,* 146–153.

Kilgard, A. K. (2009). Collage: A paradigm for performance studies. *Liminalities: A Journal of Performance Studies, 5*(3), 1–19.

Kilgard, A. K. (2011). Chaos as praxis: Or, troubling performance pedagogy: Or, you are now. *Text and Performance Quarterly, 31,* 217–228.

McLaughlin, T. (1996). *Street smarts and critical theory: Listening to the vernacular.* Madison, WI: The University of Wisconsin Press.

McRae, C. (2010). Repetition and possibilities: Foundational communication course, graduate teaching assistants, etc. *Basic Communication Course Annual, 22,* 172–200.

Pelias, R. J., & Shaffer, T. S. (2007). *Performance studies: The interpretation of aesthetic texts* (2nd ed.). New York: Kendall Hunt.

Peters, J. D. (2015). *The marvelous clouds: Toward a philosophy of elemental media.* Chicago: The University of Chicago Press.

Rice, J. (2015). Craft rhetoric. *Communication and Critical/Cultural Studies, 12*(2), 218–222.

Woodhouse, D. (2016). *Women's textile graffiti: An aesthetic staging of public/private dichotomies.* Unpublished doctoral dissertation. Southern Illinois University, Carbondale, Illinois.

CHAPTER 6

Writing and Experimentation

In this chapter, we present and consider the performance of writing as a creative pedagogical practice that can work toward moments of social justice. Using the language of performance, we discuss the pedagogical value of writing for experimentation, rehearsal, and enactment of new ideas. Performance functions as a framework for interrogating the possibilities of writing as a creative and generative pedagogical practice. A sustained writing routine is not only a practice of cultivating ideas, but also an embodied act of training the body to perform on the page. The habit of writing invites us to slow down, reflect back upon, and examine concrete experiences in ways that reveal patterns of our existence. Working from our own pedagogical use of daily writing journals and our experience writing in collaboration, we also consider the ways writing might be used to experiment with and imagine new and better ways of being in the world.

Agenda

1. Warm-up
2. Writing as performance pedagogy
3. Writing notebooks
4. Collaborative writing
5. Engagement: Writing performance
6. Closing

© The Author(s) 2017   127
C. McRae and A. Huber, *Creating Performances for Teaching and Learning*,
Creativity, Education and the Arts, DOI 10.1007/978-3-319-54561-5_6

WARM-UP

Smells like Writing

To begin this practice session, we draw on yet another embodied sense: smell. In our daily lives, how do we experience smell? What kinds of things do our olfactory senses pick up? What smells do we find pleasing? What smells do we find comforting? What smells assail our day-to-day activities? What smells do we try to avoid? What do particular smells signal for us? What smells are attached to particular events, feelings, and memories? What types of smells interrupt our thoughts, make us stop, take note, and change course? How do we make sense of the world through smell? In this warm-up, we concentrate on smell as a springboard for cultivating a writing practice. The pedagogical goal for this warm-up is to offer an exercise in which novice and seasoned writers can participate by drawing from embodied knowledge to generate written work.

Inhale.

Breathe in the smells around you.

Exhale.

Take time to smell your workspace.

With a notebook, scratch paper, or typing device at the ready, consider where you most often work. What smells pervade your workspace? Pick up the materials that surround you. Inhale their scents. Consider the books in your satchel or on top of your desk. How are the books bound? Are they new or old? How would you describe aging pages? What about other devices you use read? A tablet? A computer? A smart phone? How does each of these things smell? What odors do they emit? Jot down a few adjectives or a brief description. What do these smells bring to mind? What descriptions of these smells would you offer? Exhale.

Consider your writing utensils. Sniff the graphite in your newly sharpened pencils and the well-used rubber erasers on well-used ones. Try to breathe in the scent of your favorite ballpoint or ink pen. How would you detail these smells? Jot down a few adjectives or a brief description. What do these smells bring to mind? How would you explain what you smell? Exhale.

Consider your office supplies. Take a whiff of the correctional fluid that is solidifying in the drawer. Smell the rubber cement or crafter's glue you keep in case of emergencies. How strong are these odors? Breathe in the faint scents of paperclips, binder clips, staplers, and staples. How would you distinguish between these different metallic smells? Inhale the smell of your notebook or printer paper. Can you smell the paper? Take in the smell of the adhesive on the tape. Does it smell like your glue? Is it different? For each item, write down some adjectives or a brief description. How you would describe each smell? Exhale.

Inhale.

Breathe in the smells around you.

Exhale.

Take time to attend to the daily smells in outside your home.

Jot down a few thoughts about the smells you encounter in your everyday spaces. Consider the smells of your morning routine. Are your windows open? Inhale the breeze as it wafts through your window. Breathe in the aroma of your coffee brewing. What notes and flavors do you detect with your nose? Focus in on the other breakfast smells that surround your space. Smell the butter sizzling in the pan for your child's scrambled eggs or your partner's bread toasting. Breathe in smells of your morning fruit. What smells does the ripening banana or pear emit? Consider dish detergent you use to clean up. What perfumes does the soap employ? Consider the smells of your clothes, accessories, make-ups, deodorants, colognes, etc. Jot down a few notes or a short description about the bouquets of each. How would you explain each of these smells? Exhale.

Consider your commute to work. Do you walk or drive? What odors do you encounter on your daily journey? Consider natural and manufactured smells. Perhaps you smell rain on pavement or dried leaves on the sidewalk. Perhaps you pass by a bakery, or florist, or fishmonger's shop. Maybe from your car you can smell a factory that processes any variety of goods like oats, or meat, or soap, or paper, or tires, or hot sauce. Inhale these scents, these aromas, these stenches. As you move about your life, make note of these smells. How would you describe the each smell you detect? Exhale.

Inhale.

Breathe in the smells around you.

Exhale.

Debriefing the Warm-up

This warm-up serves as a starting place for developing a creative writing practice that is playful, imaginative, and embodied. This warm-up may be adapted and condensed for a particular group. It could also be expanded to a larger project. For instance, facilitators may encourage participants to do smell tours of particular places, or keep a smell journal over a period of time. In any case, by focusing on a particular sense, like smell, participants can write from a place of personal, embodied experience and knowledge. They can experiment with description, form, and process.

Warming-up as Embodied

The body is a site of knowledge and learning. As Taylor (2003) articulates, "Embodied practice, along with and bound up with other cultural practices, offers a way of knowing" (p. 3). In each of our previous chapters, we discuss the function of warming-up as a generative act, as a starting place for pedagogical routines, and as a practice that engages the transformative possibilities of repetition. Warming-up, in and through performance, in addition to these characteristics, is also a pedagogical practice that works to engage and consider the ways learning is always embodied. For example, the focus of the above warm-up, on the sense of smell, draws attention to the ways we learn through our bodies. Smell, like each of the senses, is a way that we come to know our world. We know by smell (we know what foods to eat, we know the presence of others, we know environmental changes and dangers, etc.). We remember through smell (we remember specific places, people, events, etc.). We learn through smell (we learn to make distinctions, interpretations, and evaluations about people, places, foods, etc.).

Warming-up, as an embodied practice, is a way to emphasize the role our body plays in our processes of learning. The senses we use and engage in our warm-up activities offer points of access for considering the ways our bodies learn. Specific senses, or other embodied practices, may be emphasized in a warm-up to match or preview subsequent lessons. For example, a warm-up that focuses on listening may precede discussions about listening, dialogue, and music. Or, a warm-up that focuses on touch may precede discussions about crafting and handmade art. In this way, warm-ups may function as an embodied preview for educational content. Warming-up can prepare participants to engage specific content in a way that is already attentive to the embodied implications of that material.

Warming-up may also be used to highlight the body as a site of learning without directly referencing questions of upcoming content or learning objectives. In other words, warm-ups are not only useful as activities that are directly linked to content. Warm-ups, especially because of their embodied nature, do not need to function as a preview or setup of some specific idea in order to be a useful starting place for engaging in any practice of learning. For example, the warm-up that begins this chapter focuses on the sense of smell which may or may not be directly related to the focus of this chapter on writing. However, this warm-up still productively functions to focus on the ways learning is an embodied practice. What is important here is that the warm-up engages and privileges the body and embodiment in learning. This prepares participants and students, even if indirectly, to consider the ways learning is always embodied and marked by embodied experience.

Writing as Critical Performative Pedagogy

As a metaphorical practice space, this book sets the stage for a range of practice sessions. The pages of this text serve as a rehearsal room, a studio, and an empty theater for holding our pedagogical ideas and experimentations: our practice sessions. Each of our sessions offers a starting place for engaging in creative practices as acts of critical pedagogy. By focusing on the critical function of creative practices, we emphasize the ways creativity can reveal the relationship between everyday acts and larger social and cultural structures. Creative practices also present the opportunity for imagining new, more socially just and inclusive, configurations of these relationships.

In the previous chapters, we offer the practice sessions of performance workshops, musical routines, and crafting practices as possible acts of critical pedagogy. These sessions also function as heuristic models for rethinking critical pedagogy. In other words, each session presents multiple openings for theorizing and enacting critical pedagogy. In this chapter, we present writing as a creative practice and act of critical pedagogy. This practice session of writing is related to three important features of the previous practice sessions. First, creative practices are generative. For example, engaging in performance workshops, musical routines, and crafting practices can yield new understandings, insights, and revelations that may or may not be related to each of these practices. Second, creative practices highlight the function and significance of routines. The structured and patterned practices of engaging in creative acts like performance, music, and crafting enable learning, improvement, and reflection. Finally, creative practices are characterized by repetition, and this repetition has a transformative function. For example, the repetition of actions in performance, music, and crafting makes each creative practice possible. A creative practice of writing is similarly generative, grounded in routine, and engages the transformative function of repetition. In this section, we make the case for a practice session of writing as an act of critical performative pedagogy.

A practice session of writing can be staged on countless surfaces including but not limited to the page, the screen, the notebook, the canvas, and the body. A practice session of writing can be enacted with a variety of tools including but not limited to pencils, pens, keyboards, paintbrushes, and crayons. A practice session of writing can occur in a range of environments including but not limited to classrooms, studios, coffee shops, parks, and libraries. A practice session of writing can take shape in different ways with different purposes, different goals, and different limitations. But a practice session of writing is always a practice that occurs at the intersection of the individual and the cultural. Writing is an individual act, and it is always a cultural performance.

Developing an individual writing practice and style is the subject of countless texts on writing. Lamott (1994) advises writers to take on short writing assignments in order to navigate the intensely personal nature of writing (pp. 16–20). She says, "Writing can be a pretty desperate endeavor, because it is about some of our deepest needs: our need to be visible, to be heard, our need to make sense of our lives, to wake up and grow and belong" (p. 19). Didion (2000) articulates the individual nature and function of writing, "In many ways writing is the act of saying *I*, of imposing oneself upon other people, of saying *listen to me, see it my way, change your mind*" (p. 17). As Harris and Holman Jones (2016) state, "words are not separate or distinct from the bodies that write, speak, and inhabit them" (p. 35). Writing is an individual and embodied act that is always implicated by personal experiences and styles.

As an individual act, writing also invites particular practices and routines. For example, Wolcott (2001) enumerates the various measures he takes before starting to write including his personal preferences for desk height, environmental conditions, and time of day (pp. 12–16). He emphasizes the importance of individual preferences for writing, and he advises: "Be discerning about the minimum conditions you require to sustain your efforts" (p. 13). Harris and Holman Jones (2016) indicate the importance of individual preferences for writers regarding space, sound, and time (pp. 1–2). And they remind, "Amidst all of this, writing is an act of performance" (p. 2).

In addition to the advice and discussion about individual writing preparations and practices, there are also countless texts offering guidance and instructions for culturally acceptable performances of writing. For example, in *The Elements of Style*, Strunk and White (1979/2000) offer cultural rules and reminders for producing good writing. Notably they instruct:

> Omit needless words. Vigorous writing is concise. A sentence should contain no unnecessary words, a paragraph no unnecessary sentences, for the same reason that a drawing should have no unnecessary lines and a machine no unnecessary parts. This requires not that the writer make all sentences short, or avoid all detail and treat subjects only in outline, but that every word tell. (p. 23)

Similar style manuals dictate cultural performances of writing grounded in principles of clarity and efficiency with an emphasis on writing that is "good." For example, Zinsser (2006) warns against clutter in writing (p. 12–16). Lasch (2002) lists stylistic characteristics of bad writing to avoid (pp. 75–92). This emphasis on clarity, simplicity, and precision as qualities of good writing are all part of a cultural expectation for a particular kind of writing. Butler (1999) reminds that the use of "difficult and demanding language" is often necessary for challenging and critiquing the status quo. In other words, clarity is not always the most appropriate or effective mode of writing. Writing, and advice on how to write, is always a cultural act.

The texts offering advice and instruction for writing present guidelines for developing and accomplishing some performances of writing. In part, these guidelines and instructions demonstrate the relationship between personal preferences and motivations for writing and cultural expectations and values about writing. These guidelines also present strategies for accomplishing writing in a particularly goal-oriented fashion. In other words, these texts all work to offer strategies for individual and cultural practices of writing designed to produce texts. Writing is certainly a performance that yields tangible products: drafts, manuscripts, notes, etc. However, writing is also a performance that can be understood as producing and constituting new ways of understanding, knowing, and being in the world. In this way, writing may be understood as a performative act that as Pelias (2005) explains works to "elicit feelings along with thought" (p. 421).

Pollock (1997) explains performative writing as evocative, metonymic/ partial, subjective, nervous, citational, and consequential (pp. 80–96). Writing as a performance that is performative enacts disruption and critique. She explains, "Performative writing is an important, dangerous, and difficult intervention into routine representations of social/performative life" (p. 75). If the performance of writing is a form of intervention, then performative writing engages and activates the critical and transformative possibilities of writing. Elsewhere, in her discussion of the performative "I," Pollock (2007) clarifies the interventionist function of performative writing explaining the performative "I" enacts: "a subjectivity grounded in an ethics of error forecasting a politics of possibility" (p. 242). Performative writing, and the writing of a performative "I," are acts that reveal the ways language and performance constitute realities and indicate ways that those realities may be constituted differently (pp. 242–243).

Performances of writing performatively are individual and cultural acts that are guided by a critical esthetics and a reflexive awareness and acknowledgment of the function of writing as performance. Spry (2011) explains, "Writing performative autoethnography is about developing one's relationship with words; it is about developing an acute awareness of the implications that language is the only thing we have between us to express the complexity of our thought and experience" (p. 99). Performative writing is a performance of writing that acknowledges and attends to the ways writing is always an entanglement of cultural and individual practices.

In an attempt to add to the extensive conversation about writing as performance (Pelias, 1999), writing as performative (Spry 2011; Pelias 2014), and writing for performance (Harris and Holman Jones 2016), we turn to the possibility of writing as an act of critical performative pedagogy. The move to position a creative practice of writing within the work of critical performative pedagogy is a move that acknowledges the function of writing in terms of performance. This move also works to understand and explain the ways writing is a practice that can be used to critically engage and learn from others and the world. We are specifically interested in offering a practice session of writing as performance pedagogy that invites play, imagination, and production.

In his extended use of the metaphors of maps and cartography to discuss writing, Turchi (2004) summarizes two related and coinciding acts of mapping and writing: exploration and presentation (p. 12). Mapping and writing entail acts of discovery and acts of presentation. The metaphor of mapping or exploration is useful for considering the ways a practice session of writing may engage in play. In her discussion of the use of a performance metaphor in theorizing teaching, Pineau (2005) describes what she calls educational play as a performative mode of engagement and critique (p. 29). She explains, "As a performative act, play enables the kinetic and kinesthetic understanding of real and imagined lived experiences, set apart from the responsibilities and culpabilities that normally attend such experimentation" (p. 27). What play makes possible in an educational context is an approach to learning that is emergent, exploratory, and embodied. In the spirit of educational play, a practice session of writing begins with an invitation to play. Writing is a performance that can be used to generate new ideas, to explore different possibilities, and to experiment with form, content, and technique.

The invitation to play in writing is also an invitation to imagine. Imagination is not separate from play; rather, it is a central feature of play that is characterized by the creation of alternative perspectives. Turchi (2004) describes the way alternative presentational maps ask the viewer to reimagine the world as "dis-orienting" (p. 102). As an example and illustration of this point, Turchi presents a map of the world that features the Southern Hemisphere on top. This inversion of traditional maps that are oriented to the Northern Hemisphere works to reimagine, and re-orient to representations of the world. Similarly, a practice session of writing presents the opportunity to generate and develop new ways of imagining and orienting to the world. Imagination enables the creation of alternative perspectives of not only the world, but also of others. As Greene (1995) argues, "imagination is what, above all, makes empathy possible" (p. 3). A practice session of writing invites imagination as a way of practicing empathy, working to create alternative perspectives, and of developing new points of contact and understanding with others.

A practice session of writing as performance pedagogy also invites production. As Turchi's (2004) mapping metaphor articulates, writing is both an exploratory and presentational act (p. 12). Writing produces texts, drafts, stories, poems, essays, autobiography, fiction, and nonfiction. Revision, editing, and rewriting are all important parts of a writing process that can aid in this kind of production of writing. However, the practice session of writing as a pedagogy of performance is also linked to the production of new ways of thinking, feeling, and being in the world and in relationship to others. The features of play and imagination that characterize a creative writing practice are linked to the production and enactment of new possibilities. These new possibilities are related to Dolan's (2005) articulation of utopian performatives. She explains:

> Utopian performatives describe small but profound moments in which performance calls the attention of the audience in a way that lifts everyone slightly above the present, into a hopeful feeling of what the world might be like if every moment of our lives were as emotionally voluminous, generous, aesthetically striking, and intersubjectively intense. (p. 5)

Similarly, a practice session of writing works to produce, in writing, the new ideas and perspectives that emerge in and through performances of play and imagination.

A practice session of writing is a kind of critical performative pedagogy that works to activate the potential of writing as a creative practice that can reveal, question, and transform the world. Warren (2011) calls for a reflexive pedagogy that works to engage the classroom, teaching practices, and classroom interactions as critical and transformative sites of research (p. 140). In his call he makes the case for teachers to engage in reflexive considerations of how they arrive at the classroom and how their values as teachers are informed by past experiences and pedagogical interactions (pp. 140–141). For Warren, research centered on pedagogical practices and histories can be transformative. In a related way, a practice session of writing takes seriously the creative process of writing as a possible site of research and transformation. Play, imagination, and production in writing can yield important and unexpected insights about the world, about others, and about us. A practice session of writing engages in the act of writing as a transformative act.

In the following sections, we discuss two examples of our use of writing as a critical performative pedagogy. First, we discuss our use of writing notebooks as a way of developing a creative practice of writing personally and in the context of the classroom. Second, we discuss the ways our collaborative efforts in writing this book inform our understanding of a creative practice session of writing. In these sections, we focus on the ways creative practices of writing can work to engage everyday experiences and practices through a process that incorporates play, imagination, and the production of new possibilities.

Writing Notebooks

Assigning students to keep a journal is not a new pedagogical practice. In our experience as students, we have been asked to maintain multiple different writing diaries to record thoughts, ideas, and observations. As teachers, we also occasionally require our students to record written work in the form of writing notebooks. These notebooks serve several functions. First, keeping a notebook encourages students to develop a routine of writing. Writing every day, or every week gets students into the habit of sitting down and putting pen to paper. Second, developing a writing notebook encourages students to attend to the process of writing. By repeating the practice of writing, students can start to see trends not only in how they write and what they notice, but how they are writing and noticing. Third, keeping a writing notebook is generative. Students not only learn what it means to craft a routine for writing, they also generate new ideas, and insights, through the process of writing.

In both undergraduate- and graduate-level classes, writing notebooks not only help students develop a habit for generating writing, they also offer a space for students to be creative and play with form, content, style. We draw from Barry's (2008, 2014) work with composition notebooks in art and writing classes to develop our own writing notebook assignments. Barry's approach encourages students to keep track of daily thoughts, observations, and insights, as well as notes for class, in various forms such as prose, poetry, narrative, illustrations, doodles, crayon drawings, photographs, and significant found materials, such as receipts, wrappers, and ticket stubs. Each semester Barry's students fill four to five composition notebooks revealing how creativity requires space for experimentation that can only be developed over time. Barry's (2014) *Syllabus* offers an example of what can be found in these notebooks, which are colorful and chaotic but also follow a set of guidelines that sustain the practice of writing.

Inspired by Barry's work, we also sustain our own personal journaling practices and assign similar writing notebook assignments in classes on writing, performance, and communication pedagogy. In addition to asking students to generate work in writing notebooks, in our classes we craft our own guidelines for daily writing, offer writing prompts, and try to get students to begin taking note of their worlds and how their perspectives inform what they write. Though the form, content, and guidelines differ from Barry's initial project, we find it helpful to assign similar writing notebook projects. In both undergraduate and graduate classes, we want students to start to cultivate habits for writing. Like Barry, we want to give students opportunities to practice documenting their daily experiences through various forms of written and artistic expression. Additionally, following Warren (2011) who encourages teachers to write up their pedagogical work, including the ways in which they theorize teaching in their classrooms and amongst themselves, we want to offer students ways to document their own strategies, theories, and day-to-day lived experiences.

Documenting lived experience not only fosters sustained writing practices, but also fosters central to our commitment to social justice and critical pedagogy. Lived experience often offers a counter-narrative to dominant texts that pervade institutional facets of life, particularly in terms of education. It is often difficult to find alternative perspectives in textbooks and other resources. However, by assigning these writing notebooks, we want students to document their lived experience as a way to both identify and transform hegemonic structures. By writing up day-to-day encounters, students can begin to recognize how they are implicated in and maintain dominant ideologies. These lived experiences can also offer alternative perspectives that resist dominant narratives, and begin to dismantle the status quo. Our hope is that by cultivating practices that document lived experience we can also begin to generate more socially just texts that are inclusive of alternative perspectives.

In what follows we offer illustrations of our experiences generating personal writing notebooks as well as examples of the writing notebooks we have assigned in an undergraduate course and a graduate course. "Writing for Performance" is an undergraduate course that presents students with the opportunity to write their own esthetic texts and to create staged performances of these texts. "Communication Pedagogy" is a graduate-level course that theorizes the communication classroom as a site for academic research. In the course, we discuss the history of communication and instruction, and survey pedagogical theories and methods. The goal of this course is to consider the philosophical and practical implications of teaching and learning communication.

Experiments with Writing Notebooks

The Writing for Performance course presents several opportunities for students to generate written manuscripts for performance. The genre, style, and content of these manuscripts are not prescribed or specified, and this lack of explicit guidelines for writing is a major challenge of the course. Students must decide what and how to write for the class. While other, less ambiguous, approaches to teaching the course, and assigning writing projects would certainly yield productive results, one goal of this open-ended approach is to privilege the performance of writing as a process with multiple possibilities (in terms of both product and method).

In order to foster this process of writing, students are assigned the task of filling two 100-page composition notebooks inspired by Barry's writing notebook assignment. Barry's (2014) guidelines for writing notebooks offer a strategy that is complementary to the challenge of the writing assignments in this course. First, these notebooks present a strategy for maintaining a daily writing practice. Barry suggests recording a daily diary entry on a single page following a specific format that includes a list of "what you did," a list of "what you saw," a quote of "something you heard someone say," and a sketch of "something you saw" (pp. 62–63). The format of these daily entries may vary; however, this basic structure works as a starting place for establishing a daily practice and routine of writing.

The second pedagogical function of these notebooks is to create an expanded expectation for writing. Barry invites the inclusion of *everything* in the notebook she explains:

> Along with diary pages, writing and drawing assignments, I'd like you to use it for work in other classes you may have, lecture notes, ideas, rants, plans, insults, first drafts of any sort on any subject, reviews. And I'd like you to include some of the ephemera from your daily life: ticket stubs, candy wrappers, receipts, labels, weird handouts, stickers, notes found on the street, torn out pictures, etc. (p. 62)

The use of the writing notebook as an archive of daily observations, and of all forms of writing works to provide a catalog that may provide multiple starting places for future writing projects. The invitation to include all forms of writing in the notebook also creates an expanded set of expectations for the ways writing might be engaged. In this way, the writing notebook functions, not only as a starting place for the creation of future texts, but as an immediate stage for practicing the daily performance of writing.

Beginning a Personal Writing Notebook

Over the summer, Chris and I have been doing a lot of talking about writing and teaching. Teaching his undergraduate writing for performance course, he assigns a series of writing notebooks, described above, which has intrigued me. I want to try to establish my own writing routine to develop my research interests and generate material for written and staged performance. I think I would like to try to keep my own journal. So we head to the local office supply store, where I purchase several composition notebooks.

Each night after our son has gone to bed, for the next couple of months. I dedicate time to working on my notebook. At first, my goal is just to write every single day. I pay little attention to Barry's guidelines for making lists, descriptions of what I hear and see, and drawings of what I experience. For pages and pages, I chronicle my own ponderings, ideas, and worries about day-to-day happenings. I describe doctor's visits, new words our one-year-old son has uttered, trips I have taken, challenges I have faced at school, and upcoming conference presentations. I write. And write. And write.

Lists, Pockets, Call Numbers

Unlike Aubrey, who rarely leaves the house without purse or satchel that can hold a larger notebook, I search for notebooks that I can discreetly keep and carry in my pockets. I experiment with crafting my own pocket notebooks, made of folded typing paper, covered with old road maps, and bound with waxed twine. I try out a variety of pocket-sized memo books that I find at office supply stores and bookstores. I discover, online, what becomes a personal favorite brand and style of 3 ½ inch by 5 ½ inch memo books that are released serially with new paperback cover designs each quarter (the colors of autumn leaves, phases of the moon, each of the fifty United States, etc.). The graph-gridded interior pages of the notebook provide the ideal stage for my daily notes.

Before heading out for the day I fill my pockets. Wallet. Keys. Cell phone. Memo book and pen or pencil. Throughout the day I fill the notebook. Usually with lists. Reminders of things to do. Reminders of things to finish. Reminders of meetings. Reminders of groceries to buy. Reminders of places to go. Reminders of stuff to pack. Reminders of deadlines. Throughout my day I cross items off the lists. And each day I recreate the lists. Adding new reminders. Rewriting unfinished reminders from the previous day. Occasionally, I write down part of an overheard conversation that strikes me as odd, funny, or otherwise worth remembering. Sometimes I jot down notes or make sketches and doodles. And every so often, when I find myself in or going to the library, I fill the pages of the memo book with call numbers for books that I hope to find.

Evolution of a Personal Writing Notebook

After taking a trip to the beach, I paste a few scenic postcards into my writing notebook. Now I have a few pictures after my pages and pages of writing, I realize my writing notebook is getting wordy. I read back over what I have written and notice is hard for me to pick out potential ideas for research or performance amongst the prose. I have begun a routine for writing, but I am worried that what I have produced will just be another diary project, one which I will eventually lose interest. Chris offers to talk to me about my writing. He explains his own writing notebook assignment and suggests that perhaps I could cease being discouraged if I would vary my method or style of working on the notebook. At the end of our conversation, he offers me Lynda Barry's (2014) *Syllabus* as an example of what he's suggesting.

From that moment on, I re-dedicate time to working on the notebook. However, instead of writing strictly prose, I work differently. I document my lists. I play with poetry. I dig out my old box of crayons and color geometric patterns and shapes. I cut out headlines and pictures from magazines and tape them to the pages of my notebook. I attach ticket stubs and receipts. My notebook begins to expand and lose its original shape as it grows with different materials. The notebook becomes a collage of my experience.

Developing a Writing Notebook Assignment: Communication Pedagogy

Based on my experience with creating a writing notebook, and hearing about Chris's assignment, I decide to assign a writing notebook for the first time in the communication pedagogy class. I think this archival practice would be helpful for graduate students to begin cultivating a routine for documenting their own teaching and learning. As Warren (2011) suggests, this type of documentation plays an important role in emphasizing classrooms and pedagogical spaces as sites for research.

I assign "pedagogy journals" in my graduate class to encourage my graduate students to start recording their day-to-day experiences in the classroom, as students and teachers. The goal is for graduate students to create a writing habit that produces narrative data of pedagogical experiences. I want them to approach pedagogical spaces as cultural ethnographers. I want them to study the classroom as a cultural site, with the pedagogy journals functioning somewhat like field notes. These pedagogy journals offer a starting place for theorizing pedagogical spaces as sites of cultural phenomena. They also provide a space in which graduate students can reflect on teaching methods, styles, and strategies, and begin to craft their own teaching philosophies.

On the first day of class, I hand each student a composition notebook and explain the pedagogy journal assignment. To develop their pedagogical journals, I ask students to record any and all "pedagogical encounters." I would like them to take time every day to work on their journals to really develop their practice and their ideas, but I only require them to have two pedagogical encounter entries a week.

These pedagogical encounters include any type of instructional moments, in which something is being taught or learned. Such encounters happen in classrooms, but often in many other spaces as well. I tell them that virtually any experience could count. Maintaining the openness of what constitutes a pedagogical encounter is important to me for two reasons. First, teaching and learning often happens beyond the boundaries of the classroom. Second, not all the graduate students in my class are currently instructors, so if all their observations have to come from classroom spaces, they can only discuss examples from classes they are taking. Students leave class twittering about what they will write in their journals, and I am excited to see what they will produce.

A Beginning

Writing notebooks are productive both in cultivating our personal writing practices and in facilitating writing in the classroom. Maintaining personal writing notebooks helps us to make time for writing, cultivate our own writing routines, and motivates us to continue to experiment with creative practices to document lived experiences. In reflecting on what we choose to document, we can also start to see how we think about the world as well as how we think about writing. Similarly, requiring our students to keep notebooks helps them develop a routine for writing, and it also asks them to attend to how writing reveals their particular perspective on the world.

Writing notebooks make space for lived experience, which can reveal dominant narratives and makes way for counter-narratives. By documenting lived experience, writers can see how they themselves maintain dominant structures of power, privilege, and access. In highlighting lived experience, and encouraging the writing to experiment with style, genre, and creative inquiry, these writing notebooks also offer space to document counter-narratives that speak against and back to what is commonly accepted as natural or normal. This practice of maintaining writing notebooks functions as a beginning for creating new performances, new practices, and new perspectives.

COLLABORATIVE WRITING

The collaborative writing project of this book offers another example of the ways a performance practice might be used to generate pedagogical insights and new teaching practices. What we learn from writing together can serve as a model for thinking about creative practices as acts of critical pedagogy. Though valuable in their own right, we argue creative practices, like writing, can also work in service of critical pedagogy. And, while there are certainly insights and strategies that we might share from our writing process about writing, what we are more interested in theorizing and sharing are the ways our collaborative performance of writing illustrate the critical value of creative practices. In other words, we are not interested, in this moment, in using our experience writing together in order to generalize instructions and strategies for ways to engage in collaborative writing projects. We believe that there are already numerous important and useful books offering writing advice. Some of these texts we reference throughout this chapter, but we do not intend to explicitly add to this body of literature. Instead, we are interested in treating our collaborative writing experience as a case study for questioning and explaining the ways collaborative and creative performances add to the development of a critical pedagogy Creative practices draw heavily on embodiment, repetition, routine, and process, which sets the groundwork for a critical pedagogical practice which reveals the ways bodies are disciplined, schooled, and made, as well as the ways world is produced, reproduced, and changed through minute ideological repetitions, routines, and processes. Our collaborative writing is a practice session for critical and performative pedagogy.

In the following section, we provide a collage of descriptive vignettes, or snapshots, of our collaborative process and performance of writing this book. In these moments of our writing, we work to show writing as a performance that is generative, that features routine, and that engages the transformative function of repetition.

Getting Started

Settling into the booth at the bakery near the campus where we work. Drinks ordered and perched next to our laptops.
Is your computer on?
Not yet.
Okay, so how are we going to start?
An online document?
That sounds good.
Can you set it up?
Yes.
Okay, my computer is on now.

The Proposal

September 8, 2015. After his Group Performance of Literature night class, Chris receives a message from his mentor Stacy Holman Jones with the flyer for the Creativity, Education, and the Arts book Series edited by Anne Harris. He writes back, "This sounds awesome ... Aubrey and I are actually working on a piece right now that includes ideas about performance, the ukulele, critical pedagogy, and arts based education." He pauses, rereads the message, and sends a second note: "I meant to say, the project Aubrey and I are working on could easily be expanded ... I'll talk to her and reach out to Anne."

An Attempted Division of Labor

"Okay, why don't you focus on writing Chap. 4, while I work on Chap. 3?"

We agree to separate the writing of these two chapters. We create two separate files. We sit on opposite sides of the room. Each of us facing away from the other. There is no need to turn and consult. There is no need to match styles of writing. There is no need to negotiate the ways these chapters are drafted. There is no need for reciprocity. There is no need to write at the same time. For two weeks, the only talk about the project is focused on our individual perceptions of the progress we are making.

I wrote about a page today.

That's good. I was stuck on this one paragraph.

That's still progress.

After about two weeks of working on our individual chapters, we both find ourselves stuck. We both find ourselves in need of help writing. We both find the attempted division of labor to be an obstacle and unnecessary barrier. We decide it is better, for us, to write each chapter together.

Walking and Writing

Without sitting in front of a computer and without committing words to paper we write and walk. On rainy days, we walk indoors. On warm days, we walk outside. As we walk we talk about our writing. We summarize sections that we have just written. We discuss the overall structure of the book. We try to imagine how our audience will interpret and receive our writing. As we walk, we worry about our words. We question our arguments. We express concern about the project. We nervously anticipate deadlines. As we walk, we write new ideas. We discuss the direction of the project. We make plans for future sections. We commit to new writing strategies. And as we walk, our writing, and our ideas, evolve and emerge.

Coffee and Tea

A ritual emerges before we sit down to write. Regardless of location (the local coffee shop, the office, the library, and our home) we both begin in a similar way every time we write together. We prepare our work surface. Laptop computers are plugged. Sweaters are donned. Notebooks and various reading materials are stacked to the side of the computers. A quick visit to our e-mail servers, social media platforms, and online news sources is made. And there is almost always a piping hot cup of coffee for Chris and tea for Aubrey.

The Script

The proposal is submitted for consideration, and within two months the writers receive positive feedback regarding the project. The script for this performance of writing emerges within the following parameters: Submit the proposed manuscript within 8 months.

The performers establish additional parameters: A specific format for writing each chapter. A more detailed outline for the book. Set writing days. Deadlines for the completion of each chapter. Goals for number of words produced daily. Goals for number of minutes spent writing each day. Accommodations for modifying these goals and deadlines based on external factors and competing obligations.

Writing Brain

It is hard to write apart just as it is sometimes hard to write together. We sit at dueling computers in our home office, or university library, or across from each other in a coffee shop, and one of us is on a writing role, fully immersed in "writing brain," tapping furiously, and taking copious notes on scratch paper or a pocket notebook. Words are coming easily, ideas are seamlessly connecting to what has come before, arguments are developing almost organically, supported by poignant examples and relevant citations. The other one has yet to get into writing brain, stuck on a sentence or idea, typing, deleting, re-reading what has come before, relenting to checking e-mail, staring blankly at the empty mug in hand.

At some point, one of us has to take a bathroom break or gets up to refill a mug, and notices how the other one is stuck. Over a beverage and usually a snack, we discuss our progress and challenges. We lay out logics and offer rationales for things that are working or not working. We brainstorm strategies for how to move forward, dismissing several before deciding on how to proceed. We talk, take notes, and sit back down.

Electricity

The table by the electrical receptacle is occupied. Their usual table. The writers frantically search throughout the rest of the dining area of the bakery for tables with access to an open receptacle. Nothing. The time available for writing is dwindling. The babysitter is only available for the next two hours. Each laptop probably has enough battery power to last for those two hours. They aren't sure. They choose a table toward the middle of the room.

One Month in the Summer

In the summer, there is one month once our teaching obligations are finished that we set time aside to travel and visit our families. We pack suitcases, we drive, we fly, and we visit. We share moments, we share meals, and we create new memories. We also pack computers, notebooks, and we bring our best intentions to work and write. But while we visit, relax, and engage with our families, we don't write. We don't work on our project. We don't discuss the direction of our ideas. And then, when our visiting is over, when we unpack our suitcases, we open the files and start again.

Problem Posing

Sitting together, we try to puzzle through ideas. We are trying to develop workshops that that we will facilitate in each of our classes. We have discussed what we need to accomplish and our rationale for holding each workshop. At this point we're stuck. We cannot seem to find a pattern to follow in order to create the overall plan. One of us gets up. The other opens a laptop, opens a blank document. She (or he) begins typing words that emerged in the conversation. She (or he) types some of the goals of the workshop endeavor. Staring at keywords and goals, a plan begins to formulate, and she (or he) types rapidly for a few minutes. The absent party returns and peers at the document. Upon seeing what has been written, he (or she) strikes up his (or her) own laptop to offer suggestion, further frame, and continue to puzzle through the format of the workshop. Collaboratively, we take to writing to work through thoughts, ideas, and possibilities.

Our individual copies of Freire's (2000) *Pedagogy of the Oppressed* are never far from our desks or our minds as we teach, research, and write. We are driven by Freire's problem-posing pedagogy in which learning is facilitated through engaging concepts through a question-based approach, which diminishes the gap between teachers as depositors of knowledge and students as receptacles of that knowledge. Instead, students and teachers collaborate to co-constitute knowledge through continuous dialogue. This approach includes grappling with problems or issues to facilitate learning. By approaching the world as a series of problems or issues to be interrogated, students and teachers come together to generate solutions based on both educational background and lived experience.

In writing together, we notice we approach writing much the same way. For us, writing is not a solitary act of knowledge production. Instead, writing is an ongoing generative project. We write to explore issues, to work through problems, and to generate potential answers, which are never fully complete or comprehensive. For us, writing is a way to learn, or rather engage in the ongoing process of learning.

Staging the Performance

Two desks on opposite sides of the room. One desk facing stage left, the other desk facing stage right. Two desk chairs, both needing to be replaced. Sunlight enters from the window, upstage.

Finding Time to Write

The cursor blinks at the end of a newly completed sentence.
The doorbell rings.
The cursor blinks at the end of a newly completed sentence.
The dinner is ready.
The cursor blinks at the end of a newly completed sentence.
Class is starting.
The cursor blinks at the end of a newly completed sentence.
Time to pick up our son from preschool.
The cursor blinks at the end of a newly completed sentence.
Assignments are waiting to be graded.
The cursor blinks at the end of a newly completed sentence.

A faculty meeting is scheduled.
The cursor blinks at the end of a newly completed sentence.
A draft of a dissertation proposal is received.
The cursor blinks at the end of a newly completed sentence.

Embodiment

A sore back.
A shift in posture.
A need to move.
A need for a snack.
An inability to fall asleep.
An inability to stay asleep.

Another New Document

I'll create a new document for the next chapter.
Okay, I'll start to fill in the outline.
Then we should talk.

Stuck and Unstuck

Inevitably, there is a passage that is difficult for one of us to finish. It has a thought that is hard to articulate. It has a feeling that is hard to convey. It has a word that just won't come to mind. One of us is stuck.

Often it is an easy fix for the other one of us. The missing word has been hiding just at the tip of the other one's tongue. The feeling is easily drafted by the one who has not been struggling with this particular series of sentences. One of us metaphorically tosses the keys to the car to the other one of us, who has no trouble getting us both unstuck.

Inevitably, there is another passage that is difficult for the other one of us to finish. And often it is an easy fix for the other one of us.

An Opening

The rough draft, the outline, the grammatical errors, the typographical errors, and the slow unfolding of ideas and thinking that happens in writing are all immediately on display. This process of collaborative writing, this iteration of working together, features an immediate vulnerability and accountability to each other. Our insecurities and uncertainty about our writing performance are on display. In part, this is a choice. We choose to work simultaneously on certain passages. We choose to write together. We choose to share in the process, rather than to isolate ourselves and to only present fully formed paragraphs and carefully constructed products of writing.

The process of working together is not entirely new for us. We often work together as performers. In performance, we are used to putting our ideas and theories on their metaphorical feet in front of each other in the context of the stage or rehearsal space. We direct, critique, and generate works in progress together. Performing, and sharing in the development of embodied performances is a process that we find familiar. However, the context of the page, and the performance of writing present new feelings of risk for each of us. Feelings of risk that might be similar to the feelings held by the students in our performance classes. Performing in front of other people can be intimidating. Preparing to perform and working through new ideas in rehearsal in front of other people can be terrifying. This kind of experimentation with others can also be immensely fruitful.

Writing together reminds us that not all acts that can be done alone should be done alone. Some seemingly solitary acts, like writing, rehearsal, or even teaching, can benefit from collaboration during and throughout the process. Opening the process of writing to each other changes our individual approaches to writing. Our writing routine emerges relationally. And our ideas, our words, our choices as writers benefit from the perspective of the other and from our own sense of shared accountability. Our collaboration serves a critical function: our individual contributions are vital for the overall project. Our individual contributions also work together, to yield a transformative set of ideas. These new, transformative ideas are something otherwise unrecognizable or impossible. Fenske (2007) working from Choi and Pak's (2006) conception of transdisciplinary collaborations explains that, "the 'trans' product of the collaboration is something both qualitatively and quantitatively different from any of the individual parts" (p. 355). The performance of writing together yields a new way of thinking, a new set of ideas, and a new way of performing and writing.

ENGAGEMENT: WRITING PERFORMANCE

Engagement Description

The primary goal of this engagement is to provide a writing practice session as a way to cultivate (or continue to develop) a routine for generating written work. The secondary goal of this engagement is for participants to experiment and play with writing. In this session, we want to offer an example of how participants might creatively approach writing as a way to continuously reimagine what a writing routine may look and feel like.

Directions/Facilitating the Workshop

Drawing from the same premise as Pelias's (2014) work in which he employs the alphabet to organize and structure produce brief performance pieces, participants will use the alphabet as a springboard to generate their own written work.

To begin the workshop, split the participants up into four to six groups, depending on the number of participants. Tell participants they will be working collectively with specific letters of the alphabet. Each group should have between five to eight letters to begin the engagement. The goal for each group is to search for and produce as many associations with each letter as possible. Depending on time and materials, encourage participants to simply make word associations, or they may extend the engagement out into developing larger two-dimensional or three-dimensional installations of such associations.

Encourage participants to use whatever is available to them, but be sure to offer time constraints to offer some boundaries to help motivate and structure their creative works. Depending on the time allotted, this part of the engagement may be tactile exercise in which participants make physical collages, or digital ones. For instance, in a similar project, participants generated word and picture associations, from doing Internet searches and snapping photographic evidence, which they then arranged in a digital file (i.e., a word document or PowerPoint slide) to be displayed on a projector. This first part of the workshop will function like a multimodal brainstorming session. If there is a theme for the session or the series of workshops, also be sure to reiterate it for the participants so that their associations may be further guided by your specific goals. For instance, in writing the proposal for this book we did this same activity, using the alphabet to generate keywords around the themes of performance, critical pedagogy, social justice, and creativity.

After the participants have created their associations with their specified letters of the alphabet, make time for each group to share their work. Encourage participants to allow the work to speak for itself, and avoid trying to explain how and why they made specific associations.

Use these initial associations as a springboard for the second part of the engagement: an individual writing exercise. Encourage each participant to choose one or two associations to develop into more fully developed written work. Designate the genre of writing (i.e., poetry, prose, advertisement, etc.) or offer participants an opportunity to develop an additional context for the association. Additionally, consider asking participants to develop a larger scene for the association that draws on personal experience or fictional storytelling.

CLOSING

A practice session of writing emphasizes writing as an embodied performance and mode of learning. The performance of writing is an act that is often linked to educational contexts in terms of producing texts, representing findings, and developing creative and imaginative ideas. By focusing on the pedagogical function of writing as a *performance*, we demonstrate the ways a practice session of writing might work to extend critical performative pedagogy. Rather than focus on the ways individual performances of writing might be refined, improved, and engaged in terms of specific cultural expectations, we turn our attention to the ways writing enacts and can transform critical understandings of the world. Writing as an act of critical performance pedagogy can work to critically engage the world, generate new possibilities, and actively produce new realities (Pineau 2002, p. 43).

As an act of critical performative pedagogy, a performance of writing celebrates the playful, imaginative, and productive possibilities of writing. The performance of writing may be characterized by the generative production of new insights and perspectives, the development of routines, and the use of repetition. And, more importantly, these characteristics may be deployed as a critical act of engaging and transforming the world. In this chapter, we present the examples of writing notebooks and our own collaborative performance of writing as possible openings for future pedagogical practice sessions of writing. These examples center on the function of writing as an embodied process with transformative potential. Other performances of writing may work toward developing a critical awareness of and attention to the world in different ways. What we hope to emphasize in our discussion of writing as a performance and act of critical performative pedagogy is the power in engaging in writing, not only to develop fixed texts, but to produce a process of interacting with and changing the world.

References

Barry, L. (2008). *What it is.* Montreal: Drawn and Quarterly.

Barry, L. (2014). *Syllabus: Notes from an accidental professor.* Montreal: Drawn and Quarterly.

Butler, J. (1999, March 20). A bad writer bites back. *The New York Times.* Retrieved from http://query.nytimes.com/gst/fullpage.html?res=950CE5D 61531F933A15750C0A96F958260.

Choi, B. C. K., & Pak, A. W. P. (2006). Multidisciplinarity, interdisciplinarity and transdisciplinarity in health research, services, education and policy: 1. Definitions, objectives, and evidence of effectiveness. *Clinical Investigative Medicine, 29,* 351–364.

Didion, J. (2000). Why I write. In J. Sternburg (Ed.), *The writer on her work* (pp. 17–26). New York: W.W. Norton.

Dolan, J. (2005). *Utopia in performance: Finding hope at the theater.* Ann Arbor: University of Michigan Press.

Fenske, M. (2007). Interdisciplinary terrains of performance studies. *Text and Performance Quarterly, 27*(4), 351–368.

Freire, P. (2000). *Pedagogy of the oppressed* (30th anniversary ed.) (M. B. Ramos, Trans.). New York: Continuum (Original work published 1970).

Greene, M. (1995). *Releasing the imagination: Essays on education, the arts, and social change.* San Francisco, CA: Jossey-Bass.

Harris, A., & Holman Jones, S. (2016). *Writing for performance.* Boston: Sense.

Lamott, A. (1994). *Bird by bird: Some instructions on writing and life.* New York: Anchor Books.

Lasch, C. (2002). *Plain style: A guide to written English.* Philadelphia: University of Pennsylvania Press.

Pelias, R. J. (1999). *Writing performance: Poeticizing the researcher's body.* Carbondale: Southern Illinois University.

Pelias, R. J. (2005). Performative writing as scholarship: An apology, an argument, an anecdote. *Critical Studies <=> Cultural Methodologies, 5,* 415–424.

Pelias, R. J. (2014). *Performance: An alphabet of performative writing.* Walnut Creek, CA: Left Coast Press.

Pineau, E. L. (2002). Critical performative pedagogy: Fleshing out the politics of liberatory education. In N. Stucky & C. Wimmer (Eds.), *Teaching performance studies* (pp. 41–54). Carbondale: Southern Illinois University Press.

Pineau, E. L. (2005). Teaching is performance: Reconceptualizing a problematic metaphor. In B. K. Alexander, G. L. Anderson, & B. P. Gallegos (Eds.), *Performance theories in education: Power, pedagogy, and the politics of identity* (pp. 15–39). Mahwah, NJ: Lawrence Erlbaum Associates.

Pollock, D. (1997). Performing writing. In P. Phelan & J. Lane (Eds.), *The ends of performance* (pp. 73–103). New York: New York University.

Pollock, D. (2007). The performative I. *Critical Studies <=> Cultural Methodologies, 5,* 239–255.

Spry, T. (2011). *Body, paper, stage: Writing and performing autoethnography.* Walnut Creek, CA: Left Coast Press.

Strunk, W., & White, E. B. (2000). *The elements of style* (4th ed.). Boston: Pearson Education (Original work published in 1979).

Taylor, D. (2003). *The archive and the repertoire: Performing cultural memory in the Americas.* Durham: Duke University.

Turchi, P. (2004). *Maps of the imagination: The writer as cartographer.* San Antonio: Trinity University Press.

Warren, J. T. (2011). Reflexive teaching: Toward critical autoethnographic practices of/in/on pedagogy. *Cultural Studies <=> Critical Methodologies, 11,* 139–144.

Wolcott, H. F. (2001). *Writing up qualitative research* (2nd ed.). Thousand Oaks, CA: Sage.

Zinsser, W. (2006). *On writing well* (7th ed.). New York: HarperCollins (Original work published in 1976).

CHAPTER 7

Future Sessions

In this final chapter, we emphasize the importance of recognizing the value of creative practices as essential for working toward social justice. In particular, we invite future sessions that articulate creative practices that exemplify and extend the connections between art and social justice. As an invitation to begin crafting future sessions, we offer several examples of everyday creative practices, which may be cultivated to generate possibilities for social justice work. In this chapter, we call for the creation of pedagogical approaches that invite imagination, creativity, process, and the room for failure. Finally, we make the case for future sessions that continue to revise, reinvent, and re-envision the practice session as a space for engaging creativity, critical pedagogy, and social justice.

Agenda

1. Warm-up
2. Practice sessions and social justice
3. Everyday performances as pedagogy
4. Creating practice sessions
5. Engagement: Future sessions
6. Closing

© The Author(s) 2017
C. McRae and A. Huber, *Creating Performances for Teaching and Learning,*
Creativity, Education and the Arts, DOI 10.1007/978-3-319-54561-5_7

WARM-UP

Tasting Performance

In each of the previous chapters, we offer warm-ups as starting places and openings for the specific practice session in each chapter. Each of the warm-ups invites some kind of a sensory engagement. Chapter 2 invites a focusing of all of the senses, Chap. 3 invites an attention to space, Chap. 4 invites the recognition of sound, Chap. 5 invites tactile awareness, and Chap. 6 invites the consideration of smell. In this final chapter, we turn to the sense of taste as an opening for thinking about and creating future practice sessions of creative and critical practices. Taste, like each of the senses, is not separate or separable from the other senses. Tasting involves and is enabled by touch. When we taste we engage our sense of smell. Tasting is also enabled and constrained by our senses of sound and sight. The pronounced intra-connection of taste with the other senses is a feature that presents a pedagogical opportunity for warming-up in a way that emphasizes, not only the specific embodied experience of taste and tasting, but of the broad ways our bodies experience, encounter, and engage the world and others.

Take a deep breath.

Exhale.

Relax your shoulders.

Imagine holding a cup of strong, black, coffee or tea. How does the cup feel in your hands? What shapes do see in the steam rising from the hot liquid? How would you describe the aroma? What does it sound like to drink this beverage? How does the first sip taste? Do you enjoy this flavor? Do you choose to keep drinking? Do you look to wash the taste away? Where are you? Who are you with?

Take a deep breath.

Exhale.

Relax your shoulders.

Imagine the smell of your favorite freshly baked pastry. How would you describe the smell of this treat? Who made this pastry? What is the texture of this baked good? What time of day is it? What time of year is it? How is the item decorated? Where are you? What does the first bite feel like? Taste like? Sound like?

Take a deep breath.

Exhale.

Relax your shoulders.

Imagine slicing into a bright yellow lemon with a sharp kitchen knife. How does the peel of the lemon feel in your hand? What is the difference in texture between the inside and outside of this fruit? Imagine the faint citrus aroma that begins to fill your space and stain your fingertips. Hold the lemon in your hand and imagine taking a bite. How does your mouth react? How does your tongue feel?

Take a deep breath.

Exhale.

Relax your shoulders.

Imagine the crunch of a salted snack like popcorn, roasted nuts, pretzels, or crackers. Imagine the salty taste on your lips and tongue. What does the snack sound like as you eat? How would you describe the texture, shape, and color of this snack? How does it feel on your fingertips? Who is with you? Are you sitting? Are you standing?

Take a deep breath.

Exhale.

Relax your shoulders.

Imagine taking a sip of water. Is the water warm, cold, or iced? What does the water smell like? Where did you get this water? From a bottle? A sink? A fountain? A hose? How does the water taste? Where are you? What are you getting ready to do next?

Take a deep breath.

Exhale.

Relax your shoulders.

Imagine sitting down to your favorite meal. What does it look like? Where are you? Who are you with? What smells fill the air? Is the food hot? Cold? How do you start eating? Do you use a utensil? Do you use your hands? What does the first bite feel like? How would you describe the taste of this food? Is it bitter? Sweet? Savory? Sour? Salty? Some combination of flavors? What does it sound like to eat this food? What sounds fill the space? What voices?

Take a deep breath.

Exhale.

Relax your shoulders.

Inhale. Focus on the smells of the space. Does the room or space smell musty? Like cleaning products? Like food? Like fresh air? Are there distinct sources of these smells? Like machinery? Like furniture? Like other people? Exhale slowly. Inhale. Focus on the smells of the space, and locate or imagine what the source of these smells looks like. What objects, relationships, and configurations are generating these smells? Exhale slowly. Inhale. Focus on the smells of the space, and identify or imagine the texture of the source of these smells. Are these smells generated by objects, relationships, or configurations that are smooth, rough, sharp, or soft? Exhale slowly. Inhale. Focus on the smells of the space, and imagine the sounds that might accompany these smells. Does the smell emerge quietly or noisily? Exhale slowly. Inhale. Focus on the smells of the space and imagine the taste or flavor of that might accompany this smell. Are the smells of the space bitter? Are they sweet? Are they sour? Are they salty? Are they savory? Exhale slowly.

Take a deep breath.

Exhale.

Relax your shoulders.

Debriefing the Warm-up

The prompts offered in the warm-up that begins this final chapter are once again centered on a sensory mode of engaging space. This warm-up asks for an attention specifically to the sensory practice of tasting, but it also recognizes the ways that all of our senses are always connected. Taste, touch, smell, sight, and sound are not separable modes of experiencing the world or others. Instead, these modes are always intra-connected. This warm-up also relies on imagination as a mode of engagement and learning. Imagination enables the creation of new connections and insights. Warming-up with imagination is also one way of starting to create and work toward new possibilities, new relationships, and new ways of being in the world. In addition to focusing on sensory experience and imagination as a way of engaging the world and others, this warm-up also offers a starting place for considering the ways warming-up works as a transformative pedagogy.

Warming-up as Pedagogy

In each of the chapters of this book, we invite you, the reader, to warm-up via various prompts and guided embodied engagements. These warm-ups are extended as examples or starting places for warm-ups that may be used in other classroom contexts. In other words, the warm-ups we present could be used directly in a variety of classroom settings (including classes that are not explicitly performance-based). Or, these warm-ups might function as a starting place for generating other ways to warm-up in the classroom. In addition to providing a set of possible classroom practices, our invitation to warm-up also draws attention to the body as a site of learning through the cultivation of routine and the use of repetition. Warming-up is a way of engaging the body, of creating a particular framework for entering spaces of learning, and engendering new possibilities for learning and relating with others.

In these ways, warming-up can be engaged as a pedagogical strategy aimed at accomplishing a particular set of goals, of setting the conditions for classroom interactions, and at establishing common ground in a variety of classroom contexts. For example, warming-up can establish a sense of community, warming-up can draw attention to and prepare the body for learning, warming-up can help with the development of focus, and warming-up can create a sense of energy and excitement. And in these ways, we believe warming-up is pedagogically invaluable. Warming-up can engender a way of learning and interacting in educational contexts that is fully engaged and embodied. However, warming-up might also be understood not only as a pedagogical tool, but as a particular kind of pedagogy.

A pedagogy of warming-up works to create a learning experience that is grounded in and features preparation and preparing as a primary educational goal and mode. As a philosophical approach to teaching and learning, a pedagogy of warming-up is committed to the idea of teaching and learning as ongoing processes. In other words, a pedagogy of warming-up does not view learning and teaching as finite acts. This is a pedagogy that values the gradual, generative, and embodied learning that happens in and through the repetition and routine of warming-up.

Practically, a pedagogy of warming-up might never move beyond the act of warming-up. This pedagogy might entail entire the dedication of entire class periods, rehearsals, and workshops to the work of warming-up. Or this pedagogy might entail a reframing of the work of entire class periods, rehearsals, and workshops *as* the work of warming-up. Rather than warming-up for some *thing* or external lesson, this pedagogy proposes warming-up as the lesson, or as the site of possible learning. A pedagogy of warming-up is a move toward re-imagining (or recognizing) the classroom as a space where realities are negotiated, constituted, and maintained. This pedagogy takes seriously the work, the interactions, and the impact of what happens in educational contexts as always consequential and immediate. Therefore, a pedagogy of warming-up is a pedagogy that is always working toward social justice.

PRACTICE SESSIONS AND SOCIAL JUSTICE

In this section, we discuss how practice sessions offer unique opportunities for social justice work. In the first part of this section, we work to define social justice as an ongoing adaptable project and process, made up of many series of acts and collaborative encounters that cultivate equity, access, and inclusion amongst individuals and in communities. In the second half of this section, we discuss how practice sessions provide an ideal setting for social justice work.

Conceptualizing Social Justice

For us, social justice means working toward establishing opportunities for those whose access and participation in social and political realms has been limited or denied. Similarly, social justice is about strategizing ways of listening to, supporting, and fostering the inclusion of these voices and ideologies into mainstream conversations, agendas, and policies. For us, social justice functions as a verb, or more accurately a gerund. It is a constant doing, working, committing and recommitting, listening and responding and, accounting for and being cognizant of power, privilege and difference. It is something to which we are always aspiring, not something that can be achieved and finished. Social justice requires a persistent commitment to working toward equity, access, and inclusion in our daily interactions. Social justice is not a destination, but a longitudinal process, that also changes over time depending on the needs of particular communities.

For us, every encounter is an opportunity to pursue social justice. As communication scholars, we believe communication constitutes the realities in which we live (Stewart 1995), which means we are responsible for and accountable to the realities created, maintained, and changed each time we open our mouths to speak, tune in our ears to listen, and use our bodies to act. This compels us to attend to our everyday communicative interactions and adapt our methods and strategies for social justice to specific interpersonal, social, and political contexts.

As historical contexts, relational circumstances, and political stakes change, the work of social justice must change as well. In our working definition of social justice, we do not want to prescribe a set action. Prescribing a particular action or series of actions limits the permeability for what may be possible in terms of social justice. Prescriptive action can also be immobilizing for those committed to establishing opportunities for equity. Instead, we want to define social justice as an ongoing, adaptable process. Social justice informs our every act, and we see each interaction is an opportunity to work toward equity, equality, and access. Therefore, it is in these mundane interludes and performances that we can strive toward social justice, and it is in these micro-moments that we can make a difference.

These micro-moments happen between individuals but are also bound to and by the communities in which they live and interact. For if, as Freire (2000), Rodriguez (2006) suggest, our individual fates are bound to our communities, then social justice must be negotiated in community relationships. Frey et al. (1996) further maintain that to "pursue justice" it is not enough to act alone; people must act together in communities to "engage and transform social structures" (p. 111). Thus, our understanding of social justice accentuated with strong collaborative component and is in line with Hytten and Adkins's (2001) assertion that "as members of the dominant culture, we cannot construct socially just educational practices alone; it is arrogant and preposterous to think we can" (p. 448).

Practice Sessions as Sites for Social Justice Work

Emphasizing routine and repetition, experimentation and creativity, and collaboration, practice sessions provide unique opportunities to work toward social justice. First, practice sessions stress the importance of developing routine and repetition. The practice session's emphasis on repetition offers participants particular opportunities to identify personal and institutional experiences with inequity. Practice sessions also engage in reflexivity about themselves and how their micro-communicative interactions contribute to, and/or maintain, and/or disrupt the status quo. Developing routines through repetition participants begin to see and experience how their personal practices are built and enhanced over time. This process encourages participants to recognize how larger social practices, ideologies, and structures are constituted over time through communicative repetitions of acts. Similarly, by attending to routine and repetition, participants begin to identify things about their personal habits, abilities, and attitudes. As they become more aware of themselves, they can also start to identify how their individual behaviors and practices are connected to larger social and political structures, maintaining, disrupting, and/or changing the status quo.

Second, practice sessions set up and maintain space for experimentation and creativity. The emphasis on experimentation affords participants with the opportunity to play, and prompts them to imagine possibilities that may not available to them in their everyday experiences. Practice sessions allow participants to not only envision, but also enact, if only momentarily, social justice. Practice sessions offer participants opportunities to engage in Dolan's (2005) utopian performance, in which, even if briefly, they can enact and participate in of the world in which they would like to live (p. 17).

Third, practice sessions require collaboration. Participants must work together to cultivate individual ideas. They must also collaborate with one another to work with thematic ideas and create larger esthetic projects. Collaboration is the foundation of practice sessions and perhaps the strongest link to social justice in that imagining and enacting equitable, inclusive practices requires community involvement and deep relational commitment. Practice sessions engage participants from various communities and develop smaller communities within the confines of the sessions themselves.

In the previous chapters, we offer practice sessions of performance, music, crafting, and writing as possible creative and pedagogical sites for social justice work. Each of these sessions emphasizes routine and repetition as pedagogically meaningful. Each of these sessions sets up and maintains space for experimentation and creativity. And, each of these sessions requires collaboration. The creative work engendered by these practice sessions is not aimed at entrepreneurial endeavors, but instead these sessions are offered as possible openings for the development and creation of new understandings and better ways of enacting the world and interacting with others. The pedagogical work of these sessions both directly and indirectly works to extend a process of working toward social justice.

The first practice session we introduce, the performance workshop, encourages the repetition and routine of embodied questioning and exploration of micro-practices and macrostructures in order to understand and reveal cultural configurations that inform and constrain our interactions and positions in the world. This session invites experimentation through the practice and process of staging theory, embodying research questions, and playing within the context of rehearsal as a means of imagining and enacting new possibilities for understanding the world and interacting with others. Finally, this session is dependent on collaboration amongst workshop participants, teachers and students, and possible audiences. Collaboration is a central feature of a practice session of performance, and it is this reliance on and requirement of interaction that offers a site for practicing and enacting communities that are inclusive and relationally committed. The performance workshop employs collaboration as a means for imagining social justice broadly, but the performance workshop also engages collaboration as a way of practicing and working toward social justice in the immediate present.

Our second practice session presents musical performance and routine as a possible creative and pedagogical process for entering into a project of social justice through the esthetic process and practice of musical engagement. First, the practice session of music emphasizes routine and repetition as epistemological structures that can be engaged in order to accomplish new ways of thinking and being in the world that might extend beyond the specific context and practice of music making. Specifically, learning to play and listen to music is a process that always implicates and is implicated by the body. The second way this practice session is aligned with a social justice ethic is the emphasis on experimentation and play. The practice session of music offers the production of music as an example of the ways exploration might yield new relationships, new sounds, and new ways of listening and making music. Finally, the musical practice session is framed collaboratively within the deeply relational context of listening. This collaborative and esthetic practice depends on the creation and maintenance of relationships with others.

The third practice session, the practice session of crafting, features a process of working toward social justice through the pedagogical process of crafting and creating handmade arts. In crafting, repetition yields the production of new esthetic objects, and this process of creation presents an analogy for thinking through the role of repetition in the process of social justice. The practice session of crafting also emphasizes experimentation and play as a method for developing new ways of thinking about and understanding the world. Importantly, this practice session is less interested in the creation of final products and more interested in developing new insights and models for making sense of the world through the engagement of artistic and artful practices of crafting. Finally, the practice session of crafting demonstrates the value and need for collaboration and interaction as a means of engaging in a creative practice. The relationships that are constituted through a collaborative process of crafting present transformative outcomes. New and otherwise unlikely processes and projects emerge through collaboration.

The final practice session, a practice session of writing, offers a pedagogical emphasis on routine and repetition, experimentation and play, and collaboration that works toward social justice in ways that are direct and indirect. A practice session of writing, like the other practice sessions presented in this book, reveals the function of repetition and routine as productive and enabling of particular acts. Repetition and routine are central features of creative practices like writing, and similarly, these are features of critical importance for a process of social justice that works to enact change. Second, a practice session of writing encourages experimentation and play in order to support new modes of writing and thinking. Finally, a practice session of writing encourages collaboration and the recognition of the ways relationships always shape and are shaped by our creative acts. In other words, although writing may seem to be an individual act, a practice session of writing demonstrates the ways this practice is always relational. The collaborative nature of a practice session of writing both exemplifies and offers an example the ways collaboration contributes to a process of social justice.

In the following sections, we outline a strategy for extending the metaphor and approach of the practice session to other everyday performances and practices that might also offer sites and conditions for work toward social justice. It is our hope that these future practice sessions and creative practices can produce ideas, relationships, and configurations that are committed to an ongoing process of enacting social justice.

EVERYDAY PERFORMANCES AS PEDAGOGY

Throughout this book, we turn to particular performances we enact and engage as possible sites of pedagogy. Performance workshops, musical performances, crafting projects, and writing are all kinds of performances that also function as sites of learning. These are acts that we engage both collaboratively and individually, and they offer examples of the ways particular performance practices might be engaged as sessions for teaching and learning. In each of the previous chapters, we consider the specific implications of each of these pedagogical acts in order to invite future engagement with each of these modes of teaching and learning. However, these examples emerge from our culturally and individually specific positions as scholars and artists, and in no way do these examples present a comprehensive view of how these performance practices might function pedagogically, nor is this an exhaustive list of possible performances that might function as sites of pedagogy.

As we turn in this final chapter toward the creation of future sessions for teaching and learning, we argue for a consideration of the ways that everyday performances function pedagogically. In this section, we call for a careful consideration of the ways all everyday performances are possible sites of learning and teaching. This call is informed by our experience theorizing our own practices, and a belief that we should not undercut, undermine, devalue, or ignore the work we are always doing as students, teachers, researchers, and artists as pedagogical. In part, this call builds off Pineau's (1995) call for re-casting the rehearsal process in creating performance as an act of research (p. 43). Though Pineau's work is specifically regarding staged performance work and the academic practice of publication, we want to similarly take seriously everyday performances as invaluable sites of knowledge and learning. In the following sections, we offer vignettes of other possible everyday performances that we enact that function pedagogically. We also provide an incomplete list of possible everyday practices and performances that might also be theorized as pedagogical. These are performances and practices that, like the performances presented in the previous chapters, could also be extended as practice sessions. What we are attempting by offering these vignettes and lists is to open the space for the consideration of multiple everyday practices and performances as sites of pedagogy. We hope to encourage through the offering of our examples you to engage your everyday performances and practices in a similar way.

Everyday Pedagogical Performance Vignette #1: Sourdough and Learning

The clear glass jar sits on your kitchen counter. Inside, an off-white mixture of flour and water is fermenting. After three days of sitting the mixture gives off the smell of alcohol and yeast. This is the beginning of a sourdough bread starter recipe. If the recipe works, there will be a living culture that can be maintained and used indefinitely for baking.

Cookbooks, Internet blogs, and video clips all provide guidance and tips for this process, but these archives of research about this particular topic don't account for the nuances and particularities of this jar of starter. There are detailed accounts and pictures about the way the fermenting water and flour should or might look. There are vivid explanations and comparisons explaining and interpreting the various smells of the starter. There are measurements and calendars describing the process. And there is learning that happens in the embodied cultivation of this fermented mixture.

Possible Everyday Pedagogical Performances Incomplete List #1: Domestic Labor

Childcare
Dusting
Grocery shopping
Letter writing
Folding laundry
Cleaning floors
Cleaning bathrooms
Paying bills
Preparing meals
Household repairs

Everyday Pedagogical Performance Vignette #2: Amateur Painting and Learning

You and your partner prepare the space for painting. You gather your tubes of acrylic paint and your blank canvases. You set out your painting tools: brushes, sponges, and a plastic fork, spoon, and knife. You squeeze some of each of the paints onto a plate: yellow, blue, red, green, white, and black. You both reach for a paintbrush and you start applying paint to the canvas. At first you are hesitant. You do not have a particular image in mind, and then, you begin to work together to create a swirling collage of colors. One of you takes a plastic fork and drags it diagonally across the entire painting. The lines left by the tines of the fork open up new blank space and create a ridge of textured color across the canvas. You both keep working and painting. You add color. You work on different sections of the canvas. You work together. You mimic techniques and gestures. You build, you change, and you revise. Gradually you create a new and unique image, as well as a new and instructive process for painting together.

Possible Everyday Pedagogical Performances
Incomplete List #2: Motion

Walking
Running
Roller skating
Ice skating
Water skiing
Bicycling
Skateboarding
Snowboarding
Sledding
Surfing

Everyday Pedagogical Performance Vignette #3:
Gardening and Learning

You decide to start growing a vegetable garden. You clear some space, you buy some seeds, and you set out to plant. You think about the direction of the sun. You consider the way the space might drain after a heavy rain. You try to map out the placement of each of the plants. You read the suggestions and instructions for planting on the back of the seed packets, and you decide to plant tomatoes, peppers, squash, and green beans. After covering the new seeds you water the ground, and then you wait. Every day, in the morning, you water and briefly check the space. After a week or so tiny sprouts start to poke through the soil. At first you aren't sure if all of the sprouts are vegetable plants or if they are weeds, but in a few days you are able to identify by the shape of the leaves that these are in fact the plants you hoped to grow. Tending to the new plants becomes part of your daily routine.

Possible Everyday Pedagogical Performances
Incomplete List #3: Outside Activities

Bird watching
Camping

Landscaping
Climbing
Shoveling snow
Hiking
Stargazing
Team sports
Swimming
Collecting seashells

Everyday Pedagogical Performance Vignette #4: Woodwork and Learning

You find plans for building a simple bookcase online. You transfer the plans into your notebook so that you can begin to better visualize how the project will come together. You measure the wall where you hope to place the new shelves and decide to slightly amend the original plans. You create a new set of plans in your notebook that accounts for this adjustment in overall height and width. You then prepare a list of needed materials. In addition to wood, you also determine that you will need a new saw blade, wood screws, sandpaper, and wood stain for finishing the project. After acquiring these items you prepare a workspace and begin making measurements for the needed cuts. Once you cut the wood, you mark what will be the inside walls of the book case in order to drill holes for the adjustable shelving. After preparing all of the pieces, you realize that you do not have enough wood for all of the shelves. One of your measurements is wrong. The project, sits unfinished for several days, before you return to the store to get the rest of the needed supplies.

Possible Everyday Pedagogical Performances Incomplete List #4: Hobbies

Stamp collecting
Scrapbooking
Model building
Jewelry making
Quilting
Candle making

Whittling
Home brewing
Gaming
Pottery

Everyday Pedagogical Performance Vignette #5: Dancing and Learning

There is music playing. The rhythms and melodies are persistent, and even though your level of expertise is minimal, you decide to dance. You move your feet. You sway your arms. You swing your hips. You spin. You sway your head from side to side. You clap your hands. You snap your fingers. You move slowly. You move quickly. You move with the music. You move against the music. Sometimes, when nobody else is watching, you dance by yourself. Sometimes you ask others to join you. Sometimes the dancing follows specific patterns and formations. Sometimes you swing. Sometimes the dancing is improvised, sloppy, and uninhibited. Sometimes you fail. Sometimes you dance in spite of yourself. Sometimes your dancing is discrete. Sometimes your dancing is proud. And each time you dance, you turn your space into a dance floor. Each time you dance you use your body to interact with and engage sound. Each time you dance you respond, you interpret, and you critique. Each time you dance you learn.

Possible Everyday Pedagogical Performances Incomplete List #5: Passions and Interests

Reading poetry
Cooking
Watching television
Hosting parties
Calligraphy
Travel
Comedy
Puzzles
Community gardening
Listening to music

Teaching and Learning Everyday

These vignettes and incomplete lists offer a starting place for recognizing everyday performances that might function pedagogically. It is important to note that these vignettes and lists, like the themes of the previous chapters, are generated from our particular cultural and individual experience and position. There are countless other everyday performances that are not mentioned here. There are countless other everyday performances that you might engage. There are also countless ways that any of these everyday performances might function pedagogically. What we hope to emphasize is not a comprehensive encyclopedia of possible everyday performances that might yield pedagogical insight, rather we hope to demonstrate the ways everyday performances might offer new ways of theorizing and enacting pedagogy. This hope is grounded in a commitment to valuing everyday performances as sites of teaching and learning.

Everyday performances and practices that could lead to pedagogical insight are infinite. Because we aim to invite the consideration of an expansive and expanding list of possible everyday performances as pedagogical, it is less important to identify characteristics that define and limit everyday acts that might function pedagogically, and instead, it is more important to note the qualities of these acts that present pedagogical opportunities. There are three qualities of everyday performances that present the opportunity for developing pedagogical insight we wish to emphasize including accomplishment, embodiment, and repetition.

First, these everyday pedagogical performances are tasks that can be accomplished individually or in groups. As a pedagogical quality, the process of accomplishing a task is more important than expertise or quality of accomplishment. For instance, in the above example of dancing, the pedagogical opportunity is not contingent on the ability of the dancer or the quality of the dance. The accomplishment of a task as a unified event or performance presents an opportunity for learning, reflection, and revelation about and through the particular performance. Dancing presents a method for learning about dancing, and about embodied learning. Dancing also presents the opportunity for reflection and revelation about the accomplishment of dance.

The second notable pedagogical quality of everyday performances is the requirement of some specialized use of the body. This embodiment may be considered passive as in the example of sitting and reading, or it may be thought of as active as in the examples of hiking and folding laundry. Regardless of the degree of engagement, the body is always implicated as a site of learning and knowledge production. Our bodies learn to enact particular everyday performances, and our bodies are marked by these performances. For instance, in the above examples of woodworking and gardening the body is changed in material ways by these practices. Hands are callused, joints are weakened, and muscles are strengthened. The embodied learning of everyday performances also presents an opportunity for reflection and revelation about the ways the performances of our bodies are always produced by and productive of cultural values and knowledges.

The third quality of everyday performances that presents pedagogical insight is the repetition of specific actions or patterns of actions. For example, the performance of cooking might entail the repetition of specific actions like cutting, or patterns of action like preparation, sautéing, and stirring. Repetition, in the actions of everyday performances, functions to create, maintain, and transform the meanings and effects of these performances. Repetition can also conceal and reveal insights about the ways cultural meanings and values are produced. Pedagogically, repetition in everyday performances presents an important opportunity for consideration about the ways performances participate in cultural formation, and could participate in cultural transformation.

Accomplishment, embodiment, and repetition are not the only possible pedagogical qualities of everyday performances. However, these characteristics present a starting place for extending and attending to everyday performances as critical and creative pedagogical acts. In the following section, we trace a path for theorizing everyday performances as practice sessions for teaching and learning.

CREATING PRACTICE SESSIONS

In this section, we argue the practice session metaphor offers a guiding structure for theorizing everyday practices as pedagogical acts. We then offer practical applications for practitioners and educators to create their own practice sessions. We begin by articulating the importance of the practice session as the structuring frame for pedagogy, based on the significance that practice sessions place upon everyday lived experience and practice sessions' potential for disrupting transactional models and modes of learning.

Practice Sessions: A Structure for Pedagogy

First, practice sessions highlight the inclusion and generation of everyday lived experience as a site of knowledge production. Identifying everyday performances as possible practices of teaching and learning is work that takes seriously the possibility for pedagogy to emerge in and from multiple experiences and contexts. This work asks the question: What are everyday performances that I engage? What are everyday performances that I take-for-granted? What everyday performances might offer important pedagogical insights? Theorizing these everyday performances as pedagogical practice sessions moves beyond the recognition that learning happens in our everyday performances and toward a systematic appreciation and engagement of the possibilities of that learning. In other words, creating practice sessions from everyday performances works to engage everyday performances as new ways of thinking about and practicing pedagogy. Creating practice sessions from everyday performance asks: How might a specific everyday performance provide a model for teaching and learning? How might a specific everyday performance present the possibility for a pedagogy of critique or transformation? How might a specific everyday performance modify existing pedagogical approaches and assumptions?

The process of creating practice sessions from everyday performances attempts to engage acts that might be otherwise taken-for-granted as pedagogically meaningful and generative. Everyday practices always emerge from individual and cultural experiences and expertise. Creating practice sessions from everyday practices is an act that privileges and values the varied critical insights and embodied knowledge of these cultural and contextual practices. By focusing on everyday lived experience, practice sessions offer alternatives to traditional education practices in which people other than students, and often teachers, set curriculum and what is understood and counted as knowledge.

Second, creating practice sessions and pedagogies that extend, apply, and attend to the pedagogical value of everyday practices and lived experience is an act that works to disrupt and expand transactional models and approaches to teaching and learning. Practice sessions engender a collaborative learning environment and practice. Students must be actively involved in offering examples questioning practices, and generating and receiving feedback to produce co-constituted knowledge. They are not passive vessels to simply retain and accept what they are told. Instead, teachers (or facilitators) and students (or participants) must work together to develop expectations, cultivate approaches, methods, and routines, and generate collaborative projects. In the following "frequently asked questions" section, we discuss how future educators and facilitators may begin to develop their own practice sessions.

FAQ (Frequently Asked Questions) for Creating Practice Sessions

Q: How would I go about developing a practice session?

A: First, consider your goals, expertise, participants, and aptitude for ambiguity. Though carefully thought-out and planned, the outcomes of practice sessions cannot be fully anticipated. Begin planning your session around a goal or theme and group of participants. In terms of method, do not be afraid to step outside your comfort zone. Part of creating practice sessions is learning how to engage in the creative process.

Q: What would a general practice session format look like?

A: You can format your practice session based on your own needs and context. As teachers, we find it productive to organize the practice session in a similar format to how we might organize a lesson plan for our classes. We begin with an overview or an agenda that outlines the events of the session. We then develop a warm-up that previews the main themes of the session and engages one or more of the participants' embodied senses. We also try to debrief the warm-up so that participants understand how it is connected to our overall theme.

After the warm-up, our practice sessions include some sort of theoretical framing for the theme of the practice session, complete with practical applications. This piece functions as background for why and how the theme of the session is important in a particular context or contexts. This theoretical framing may consist of a lecture-like description or a series of explanations and exercises for participants.

In addition to providing some background about the theme of the session, we also want to offer participants with a way to deeply engage the theme, so we also generate an extended engagement or activity in which participants work collaboratively and/or individually to apply ideas and perhaps generate new ones. Finally, in each session we find it important to offer a summary of the session in order to synthesize ideas, activities, and propose future directions.

Q: How long does each part of the session take? For example, how long would you spend on the warm-up?

A: Each piece of the practice session can be adapted to an individual workshop or class, or be condensed to fit in a more limited time period depending on the goals for the session. Often the theoretical framing and engagement pieces of the session take the majority of the time. Warm-ups and debriefing usually take between 5 and 15 min. In addition to engaging the senses, the warm-ups tend to function as a preview for the session

Q: Does the engagement require a singular project to be accomplished?

A: The engagement may focus on a singular project or goal and typically does result in the accomplishment of a particular project. The engagement can also serve as part of a larger process or project. For instance, in a performance setting, we might generate multiple sessions that work with different themes such as scripting, music, production concepts, and embodiment. The engagements from each of these sessions could work together to produce various parts of a larger production. We might also create practice sessions in which the engagement works more with ideas or fragmented pieces to apply, identify, or expose different perspectives and deep understandings of a particular theme.

Q: How do you understand everyday performances as pedagogical?

A: We understand everyday performances as pedagogical in that they are opportunities for teaching and learning. Not only do we learn how to enact everyday performances, we also learn *by* engaging in these activities. A pedagogy of everyday performances considers and takes seriously the educational value and method of any given everyday performance. It is not necessarily the everyday performance itself that is important here; it is how and what the everyday performance teaches (about learning, about the world, about others) through its practice. Everyday performances present possible models for creating new and different philosophies of teaching and learning.

Q: How can I take an everyday performance and turn it into a practice session?

A: You will want to consider what you have learned by engaging in the everyday performance. What kind of learning takes place when you engage in the everyday performance of cooking or gardening or listening to music? You have probably learned something about the practice itself. For instance, engaging in various everyday performances of cooking, we have each learned efficient and safe ways of cutting, slicing, and dicing, various fruits, vegetable, meats, and cheeses. You have also probably learned something about your learning style or how you are able to learn. For instance, in learning and practicing the ukulele, Aubrey has learned she often needs to see an example on sheet music, as well as have a model (in which she watches someone else play) before she really can play a new strumming pattern herself.

In addition to considering what you have learned about the practice and what you have learned about your particular learning style, you want to decide on what element of that everyday performance you want to develop into a practice session. That is to say, you want to determine how you will translate your own experience into a larger session for others. For instance, do you want participants to learn something about the practice itself, or is your goal to try to highlight the type of learning that happens when engaging in that practice? For instance, in our chapters on musical practices and crafting, we wanted to draw participants' attention to the ways in which repetition and routine reveal particular insights about individual and social experience.

Next, consider the ways you might develop your practice session around your primary goals. What do you want to highlight or work with in your workshop? What does the particular everyday performance bring into focus? Is it something about a concept like routine, repetition, ideology, or cultural values? Or does the everyday performance reveal or point to a more specific question such as ethical food practices or empathy? It is helpful to begin by developing and articulating your goals so you can identify the overall direction of the practice session. You can then also draw on particular aspects of the everyday performance to further develop the warm-up and engagement so that participants can apply and embody the goals of the session.

Q: Does a practice session need to take place in a traditional classroom context? Who are possible students for practice sessions?

A: Practice sessions encompass traditional classroom contexts, but they are not limited to those contexts. We use the label practice sessions to expand what a pedagogical location or context might look like.

Practice sessions can be formatted for any setting in which learning takes place. You could develop practice sessions in conjunction with classroom and workshop practices, or as part of a program for organized civic or social groups and clubs. One could also organize practice sessions as part of one-on-one and group lessons, tutoring, and impromptu gatherings. Practice sessions can and should include a variety of settings in which people come together and learn from and with one another.

Q: Do we need to make the link between practice sessions and social justice explicit?

A: For us, practice sessions open up space to work toward social justice. Bringing people together to identify and work with personal and social communicative practices that constitute the world opens the door for social justice pedagogy. However, we do not mean to say that social justice is as easy as gathering people together. To work toward enacting social justice, attention must be drawn to process and how the world is developed and created through repetitions of communicative acts. Similarly, facilitators and participants must be committed to experimenting with new ideas and possibilities to reimagine how the world could be. They must also be dedicated to a collaborative effort in order to realize and enact change. This may mean articulating specific social justice aims, or it might mean developing these aims together as a group throughout the process of the practice session.

ENGAGEMENT: FUTURE SESSIONS

In this final engagement, rather than provide the outline of a possible format or set of guidelines for creating a particular session of your own, we offer a letter as another possible form of engagement. In particular, we work to engage you, the reader, in our call for future sessions as enactments of creative and critical pedagogy that works toward and on behalf of social justice.

Engaging Future Sessions

Dear Reader,

As this book comes to an end, we write you with a note of thanks and a request. First, we want to thank you for joining us in this series of lessons, warm-ups, and engagements. We value the relationships that are created in educational contexts; though this book does not function entirely in the same way as a traditional classroom, it does present the possibility for the emergence of new relationships. These relationships and points of contact and connection matter. These relationships are the site of learning and transformation. These relationships are critical. Your relationship with us, even as we strive to imagine you, has transformed us, and we are grateful for this opportunity. Even if we never meet you off the page, we want to acknowledge that you reading and engaging with our ideas and suggestions matters to us, and we appreciate your participation.

Second, we want to ask for your consideration and participation in this project of creating and engaging the metaphors of practice spaces and sessions as you develop your own approaches to teaching and learning. When we set out to write this book, we began by reflecting on our individual and collaborative creative practices, endeavors, and experiments as possible sites of critical pedagogy. Some of the practices were already directly located in educational contexts and our educational practices. For example, we both teach classes in performance studies, and we frequently employ performance workshops as ways of organizing and engaging the content of the classes we teach. However, some of our other creative practices were not related to our pedagogy or even our research. For example, our crafting projects and musical experiments were not directly related to our scholarly commitments to critical pedagogy and social justice. Or, at least that's what we thought. Then we started to realize and recognize the ways these creative practices were not only relevant to our research interests and pedagogical approaches, we also realized that these practices already informed the ways we approached and thought about teaching and learning. The embodied lessons and techniques of our creative practices always shape the ways we think about and practice teaching and learning as a dynamic, relational, and emergent process.

Throughout this book, we work to articulate the connections between our creative practices and our approach to critical pedagogy. We believe that the generative, experimental, repetitive, reflexive, and embodied characteristics of creative practices can be meaningful for the development of critical approaches to pedagogy. Creative practices present an opportunity for new and better ways of thinking and being in the world and with others. We also work to specify creative practices as sites of critical pedagogy and social justice, and this is where we turn to you with our request and call for future practice sessions. The creative practices we outline in this book (performance workshops, music, crafting, and writing) are not comprehensive, nor is our treatment of the four creative engagements we discuss. We hope that you might extend and transform our proposed metaphor of practice sessions by developing and articulating your own creative practices, and your own ways of practicing creative engagements, as acts of critical pedagogy.

The practice session metaphor provides an organizing structure for applying creative practices in pedagogical contexts. Practice sessions occur in a given period of time, they happen in a given location, they follow certain patterns and routines of action and activity, and they often use repetition as a strategy for teaching and learning. We believe the structure of the practice session is applicable to a wide range of practices. However, in order to activate this metaphor, creative practices are needed. So, what are your creative practices? What embodied and sensory performances do you engage? What activities do you practice as a student? When do you collaborate? And if the practices we include in this book are also your practices, how do you engage in these acts?

Of course we hope that our practice sessions can be productive and generative for you. We hope that you will try the engagements we offer here, but we also want you to develop your own practice sessions that emerge from your daily lives and lived experiences. We want you to engage your own creative repertoire as a rich site for thinking about and theorizing pedagogy. We want our practice sessions to mark an opening for multiple future practice sessions for pedagogy.

Attending to the practices that we already in engage in our daily lives as pedagogical acts works to acknowledge the ways our pedagogical and scholarly commitments are always also shaped by our personal experiences. In other words, it is our belief that our everyday practices inform the ways we think about and practice teaching. This idea is not necessarily novel, but we want to emphasize the pedagogical value and importance of practices and performances that we might otherwise take for granted. Your everyday practices and performances are potentially invaluable to understanding, theorizing, and transforming your pedagogical work.

We also think that our everyday practices might do more than just shape our pedagogy; we think that we might begin to engage these everyday practices as a kind of pedagogical framework. How might your everyday performances serve as pedagogical model? How might you extend these performances to other educational contexts? We want to draw attention to everyday practices as pedagogical in order to expand and extend conceptions about the site and practice of teaching and learning. We offer the practice session metaphor to you as a way of foregrounding your embodied knowledge and everyday practices in the creation of your own teaching and learning.

Turning everyday performances into pedagogical practice sessions might yield particular activities and forms of engagement in classroom contexts. Or, you might develop new organizing frameworks and structures for approaching content and specific lessons based on the structures and frameworks of particular everyday performances. Everyday performances might offer analogies, metaphors, or heuristics for developing and theorizing pedagogy, classroom interactions, and critical scholarship. We want to also acknowledge that the practice session metaphor might also fail. It might come up short or prove inadequate as a way of linking the pedagogical insights of everyday performances with other educational contexts. In these instances, we hope for revision, reinvention, and re-envisioning of the practice session metaphor. Our ultimate goal is not to present a finite pedagogical strategy. Our goal is to continue finding ways to bring creative practices in conversation with the work of critical and social justice pedagogies.

We hope this project can be continued and expanded by the inclusion of your practice sessions. We are curious to learn what might happen next, how the practice session might engender a space for engaging creativity, critical pedagogy, and social justice. And we are determined to continue engaging and advocating for creative approaches to pedagogy as critical and transformative acts.

Yours,

Chris and Aubrey

Closing

In this final chapter, we encourage a consideration of the pedagogical implications of everyday performances and practices as one possible starting place for developing future pedagogical practice sessions. We turn to everyday performances and practices because these acts are creative, generative, and most often taken-for-granted as sites of learning. Everyday performances emerge pedagogically. These practices are taught and learned. These are practices that teach, provide insight, and shape relationships. Everyday performances are possible sites of creativity. Things are made, ideas are developed, materials and matter are transformed. Everyday performances present a critical pedagogical opportunity. These performances present the opportunity for creating and enacting social justice through routine and repetition, experimentation and creativity, and collaboration. These performances present the opportunity for learning, for connection, and for new ways of being.

Our turn to everyday performances is offered as a way of extending an invitation for continued development of practice sessions as ways of enacting critical and creative pedagogy. Calling for everyday performances as sites of future practice sessions is less about specifying what kinds of acts might be pedagogical and is more about a move toward the inclusion of a diverse range of emergent pedagogical sites. In terms of Conquergood's (1995) metaphor for performance studies as a caravan, we are interested in marking the practice session as an approach to creative and critical pedagogy that is "a heterogeneous ensemble of ideas and methods on the move" (p. 140). We offer the practice session as one way of working toward engaging creative practices as pedagogical and critical acts.

The practice session is an event that privileges the learning that happens through repetition and revision. The practice session is a type of pedagogical performance that offers both a way of knowing and a way of being. This is a pedagogical performance that privileges the process of coming to knowledge from multiple directions. This is a pedagogical performance that works to constitute reality, to develop techniques, and to reflect and revise ways of being in the world and with others. The practice session and future practice sessions are pedagogical performances that engage in creative acts and embodied performances in order to generate more socially just configurations and understandings.

Future practice sessions may emerge from everyday performances, or they may emerge as revisions of or additions to the practice sessions offered in this book. Future sessions may borrow, extend, or rethink and repurpose the metaphor and structure of the practice session. Our hope is that future practice sessions continue the project of engaging creative work as pedagogical work. Creative work, creative acts, creative performances are important sites of learning and teaching. Our hope is that future practice sessions embrace the pedagogical potential of creative work as work that is not only productive, but that is also always critical and transformative.

REFERENCES

Conquergood, D. (1995). Of caravans and carnivals: Performance studies in motion. *The Drama Review, 39*(4), 137–141.

Dolan, J. (2005). *Utopia in performance: Finding hope at the theater.* Ann Arbor: University of Michigan Press.

Freire, P. (2000). *Pedagogy of the oppressed* (30th anniversary ed.) (M. B. Ramos, Trans.). New York: Continuum (Original work published 1970).

Frey, L. R., Pearce, W. B., Pollock, M. A., Artz, L., & Murphy, B. A. O. (1996). Looking for justice in all the wrong places: On a communication approach to social justice. *Communication Studies, 47,* 110–127.

Hytten, K., & Adkins, A. (2001). Thinking through a pedagogy of whiteness. *Educational Theory, 51*(4), 433–450.

Pineau, E. L. (1995). Re-casting rehearsal: Making a case for production as research. *Journal of the Illinois Speech and Theatre Association, 46,* 43–52.

Rodriguez, A. (2006). Social justice and the challenge for communication studies. In O. Swartz (Ed.), *Social justice and communication scholarship* (pp. 21–34). Mahwah, NJ: Lawrence Erlbaum Associates.

Stewart, J. (1995). *Language as articulate contact: Towards a post semiotic philosophy of communication.* Albany, NY: Suny Press.

INDEX

A

Absences and presences, 21, 22
Adkins, A., 161
Aesthetic texts, 101
Agenda, 8
Alexander, B.K., 3, 28, 46, 47
Arnett, R., 62
Artz, L., 161
Atmospheric attunement, 21
Autoethnography, 28, 134

B

Banking model of education, 32
Barad, K., 89
Barry, L., 137, 139–141
Barthes, R., 106
Bell, E., 61
Blair, J.M., 113
Boal, A., 19, 48, 63
Body, 19, 20. *See also* Embodiment
  as cultural, 24
  and pedagogy, 30
Bogart, A., 48, 68
Bottoms, S., 48
Bowman, M.S., 48, 52

Bowman, R.L., 48, 52
Bresler, L., 83
Brownlee, S., 114
Butler, J., 24, 89, 133

C

Cadiff, Janet, 22
Carnal coefficient, 22
Certeau, M.de., 36
Choi, B.C.K., 150
Classroom
  and possibility, 12
  relationships, 12
  as sites of cultural production, 5
  space, 37–40
Collaboration, 7, 127, 161, 162. *See
  also* Writing and collaboration
Collage, 103–105
Communication, 23, 29–31, 72, 160.
  See also Listening
Community, 43, 48, 50
Conquergood, D., 23, 24, 56, 57, 62,
  106, 180
Contact, 56, 57
Cooks, L., 28

Crafting, 151. *See also* Collage
  as activism, 102
  and card-making, 106, 107
  as critical pedagogy, 101, 103, 104, 106, 111
  and repetition, 106, 107, 119
  and stop-motion animation, 112–115, 117–119
  workshop, 120–123
Creativity, 5, 11. *See also* Creative pedagogy; Social justice and creative practice
  creative practice, 5, 19
  process-focused creativity, 26
Cultural position, 47
Cusick, S., 76

D
Deaton, C.M., 113, 114
DeChaine, D.R., 82
Dialogic engagement, 57
DiAngelo, R., 29
Didion, J., 132
Dolan, J., 24, 57, 66, 136, 162
Double articulation, 60

E
Educational play, 25, 135
Educational poetics, 25
Educational power, 25
Educational process, 25
Ekphrasis, 106
Embodiment, 8. *See also* Warm-up as embodied
Empathy, 57
Engagement, 8
  examples, 40, 45, 84, 97, 106, 112, 124, 136, 138, 142, 146, 152, 153, 155, 158, 164, 165, 170, 172

Esthetic texts, 57
Ethnography, 27, 56. *See also* Performance ethnography
Exaggeration, 52, 55
Experimentation, 40. *See also* Routine
Explanation, 52, 53
Exploration, 52

F
Fassett, D.L., 27, 29, 32
Fenske, M., 150
Féral, J., 22
Freire, P., 26, 31, 32
Frey, L.R., 161

G
Geertz, C., 28
Generative autobiography, 46, 47
Generative performance response, 47
Gingrich-Philbrook, C., 90
Goulish, M., 48
Grande, S., 27
Greene, M., 135
Greer, B., 102

H
Hall, S., 60
Hamera, J., 23, 31
Harris, A., 26, 31, 87, 132, 134
Holman Jones, S., 77, 106, 132, 134
Huber, A., 52
Hytten, K., 29, 161

I
Image work, 63–66
Inclusivity, 3
Interaction, 48–50
Ivashkevich, O., 113, 114

J
Johnson, E.P., 77
Johnson, M., 32
Juxtaposition, 103, 119, 124

K
Kamp, B.L., 113, 114
Kassabian, A., 75
Kilgard, A., 36, 103–106, 114, 120
Kincheloe, J., 27, 29, 63
Koza, J.E., 77, 87
Kun, J., 83

L
Lakoff, G., 32
Lamott, A., 132
Landau, T., 48, 68
Langer, S.K., 77
Lasch, C., 133
Learning space, 37. *See also*
    Pedagogical context
Leder, D., 21, 89
Lesson plan, 7
Levinas, Emmanuel, 62
Listening
    adequate, 74
    modes of, 74, 75
    musical listening, 92, 94, 163
    perceptual agency, 83
    performative, 75
    ubiquitous, 75

M
Macro-structures, 57, 60, 62, 63
Madison, D.S., 3, 52
McLaren, P., 27, 81
McLaughlin, T., 102
McRae, C., 32, 52, 71, 75–77, 83,
    94, 108

Metaphors, 32, 33
Micro-practices, 57–60, 62, 63, 162
Monson, I., 83
Murphy, B.A.O., 161
Music, 10, 74. *See also* Listening;
    Routine
    as critical pedagogy, 71, 72, 76,
        78–80, 82
    as cultural, 74, 76, 78, 81, 86
    as embodied, 71, 76–78, 80–82
    learning to play, 85–91
    musicking, 76

N
Nainby, K., 83

P
Pak, A.W.P., 150
Pascoe, C.J., 27
Pearce, W.B., 161
Pedagogical context, 37
Pedagogy, 9, 78, 103, 131. *See also*
    Crafting as critical pedagogy;
    Music as critical pedagogy;
    Performance and critical pedagogy;
    Writing as critical performative
        pedagogy
    chaos, 114
    creative pedagogy, 24, 26
    critical communication pedagogy,
        27, 28
    critical pedagogy, 23, 26, 27, 63, 66
    critical performance pedagogy, 2–4
    critical performative pedagogy, 2, 3,
        30, 31
    dialogic approach, 32
    everyday performances, 164, 165,
        170
    performative pedagogy, 78
    Pedagogy of the Oppressed, 26, 148

Pelias, R.J., 23, 24, 48, 54, 101, 121, 134, 151
Performance
  as creative mode of inquiry, 4, 5
  as creative pedagogy, 24
  and critical pedagogy, 23
  definition, 23, 25
  ethnography, 56
  as research, 43, 52, 63
  and social justice, 4, 5
  study of, 27
  theory, 12
  workshop, 48–57, 59, 61–65
Peters, J.D., 90, 101
Pineau, E.L., 2, 18, 20, 25, 30–32, 48, 52, 81, 135, 152, 165
Pineda R.D., 77
Poetics of the oppressed, 19
Pollock, D., 134
Pollock, M.A., 161
Power, 63, 102, 143
Practice session
  definition, 15
  format, 7
  metaphor, 6, 32–34, 135, 164, 171, 177
  method for generating performance and pedagogy, 6, 137
Practice space, 5, 15, 33, 35–37, 39, 40
Privilege, 54, 62, 63, 86, 87, 91, 102, 143

R
Reflexivity, 62, 94, 161
Repetition, 5, 163. See also Crafting and repetition; Writing and repetition
Research, 9. See also Performance as research
Rice, J., 103
Rodriguez, A., 161

Routine, 71, 72, 74, 78–84, 159, 161, 164. See also Writing and routine

S
Senses
  sense of sight, 21
  sense of smell, 21, 130, 131
  sense of sound, 17, 21, 83, 85, 86, 91
  sense of taste, 21
  sense of touch, 21, 100, 114, 123, 124
  sensual experience, 20
Sensoy, O., 29
Shaffer, T.S., 48, 54, 101, 121
Shoemaker, D., 77
Simmons, J., 90
Small, C., 76
Smellwalks, 21
Social justice
  and creative practice, 164
  critical, 29
  and pedagogy, 4, 25, 30
  and performance, 4, 161
Soundwalking, 21
Space, 36, 157
Spry, T., 48, 77, 134
Stewart, J., 32
Stewart, K., 21
Stinson, S.W., 82
Stockfelt, O., 74
Structure, 57. See also Macro-structures
Strunk, W., 133
Stucky, N., 18
Sudnow, D., 80

T
Taylor, D., 24, 130
Teaching as performance, 18
Transformation, 63
Turchi, P., 135

U
Ubiquitous, 75
Utopian performative, 136

V
VanOosting, J., 23
Vernacular theory, 102

W
Walser, R., 77
Warm-up, 8
  as embodied, 130
  examples, 40, 45, 97, 124, 152, 155
  as generative process, 46
  pedagogy, 16, 153
  performance, 18
  as repetition, 100
  as routine, 74
  senses, 21
Warren, J.T., 20, 27, 29, 32, 78, 81,
    136, 138, 142
Westerkamp, H., 21
White, E.B., 133
Willis, P., 27, 81

Wimmer, C., 18
Wolcott, H., 132
Woodhouse, D., 102
Workshop, 9, 97. *See also* Crafting
    workshop; Performance workshop
Writing
  and collaboration, 150
  as critical performative pedagogy,
    131, 136
  cultural rules, 133
  as generative, 130
  and mapping, 135
  notebooks, 137
  as performance, 146
  performative writing, 134
  practice and style, 132
  and repetition, 124
  and routine, 132, 139

Y
Yordon, J.E., 48

Z
Zinsser, W., 133

Printed by Printforce, the Netherlands